Israel and Palestine

Peace Plans and Proposals from
Oslo to Disengagement

Israel and Palestine

Peace Plans and Proposals from Oslo to Disengagement

Galia Golan

Markus Wiener Publishers
Princeton

For information write to:
Markus Wiener Publishers
231 Nassau Street, Princeton, NJ 08542
www.markuswiener.com

Library of Congress Cataloging-in-Publication Data

Golan, Galia.
  Israel and Palestine : peace plans and proposals from Oslo to disengagement / Galia Golan.
    p. cm.
  Includes bibliographical references and index.
  ISBN-13: 978-1-55876-420-0 (hardcover : alk. paper)
  ISBN-10: 1-55876-420-8 (hardcover : alk. paper)
  ISBN-13: 978-1-55876-421-7 (pbk. : alk. paper)
  ISBN-10: 1-55876-421-6 (pbk. : alk. paper)
  1. Arab-Israeli conflict--1993---Peace. I. Title. II. Title: Peace plans and proposals from Oslo to disengagement.
  DS119.76.G615 2006
  956.9405'4--dc22   2006023961

Printed in the United States of America on acid-free paper.

Contents

LIST OF MAPS VII

ACRONYMS IX

CHAPTER ONE
Introduction I

CHAPTER TWO
The Oslo Accords, 1993–1999 9

CHAPTER THREE
Camp David July 2000 37

CHAPTER FOUR
The Clinton Parameters—December 2000 49

CHAPTER FIVE
Taba—January 2001 55

CHAPTER SIX
Mitchell-Tenet-Zinni Recommendations—April 2001–March 2002 63

CHAPTER SEVEN
The Saudi Initiative-Arab League Resolution and UNSC Resolution 69

CHAPTER EIGHT
President Bush: October 2001—The Rose Garden Speech June 2002 73

CHAPTER NINE
The Road Map—30 April 2003 77

CHAPTER TEN
The Geneva Accord—October 2003 93

CHAPTER ELEVEN
The Nusseibeh-Ayalon Petition (The Peoples' Voice)—July 2002 113

CHAPTER TWELVE
The Disengagement Plan—2003–2005 119

CHAPTER THIRTEEN
U.S.-Israel Understandings: Bush and Weissglas Letters. 131

CHAPTER FOURTEEN
Conclusions: Is There a Plan for Peace? 137

EPILOGUE 143

POSTSCRIPT 149

NOTES. 151

APPENDIX I
Letters of Mutual Recognition 165

APPENDIX II
Declaration of Principles 169

APPENDIX III
Beirut Summit 185

APPENDIX IV
Road Map. 189

APPENDIX V
Geneva Accord—A Model Agreement 199

APPENDIX VI
Sharon's Disengagement Plan 209

APPENDIX VII
U.S.—Israel Understandings .217

INDEX 225

Maps

Oslo II Redeployments (1998 to present). 22

Israeli Proposal at Camp David Summit 40

Jerusalem: 1949–1967 43

The Old City of Jerusalem 44

Map Reflecting Clinton Ideas 51

Israeli Proposal, Taba 2001 58

Geneva Initiative: Israeli-Palestinian Permanent Borders 98

Gaza Strip 120

Northern West Bank 121

Israeli Settlements and Outposts—2006 128

The Separation Barrier—August 2006 134

Acronyms

CIA	Central Intelligence Agency
DFLP	Democratic Front for the Liberation of Palestine
DOP	Declaration of Principles
EU	European Union
IDF	Israel Defense Force
IVG	Implementation and Verification Group
MF	Multinational Force
PA	Palestinian Authority
PFLP	Popular Front for the Liberation of Palestine
PLO	Palestine Liberation Organization
PNC	Palestinian National Council
TIP	Temporary International Presence
TIPH	Temporary International Presence in Hebron
UN	United Nations
UNGA	United Nations General Assembly
UNSC	United Nations Security Council
UNRWA	United Nations Relief and Works Agency

CHAPTER ONE

Introduction

The Arab-Israeli conflict is often characterized as an "intractable" conflict, so long and often in the news, so long and often the subject of debate, and so often the object of failed attempts at solution, that conflict management rather than resolution might be the more appropriate approach. In contrast, however, a number of elements of the conflict have in fact been resolved. There is an Egyptian-Israeli peace agreement over twenty-five years old that has withstood the strains of an Israeli invasion of an Arab country (Lebanon 1982) and has succeeded to the point that Israel has actually sought a military as well as political Egyptian presence to assist in Israeli withdrawal from occupied territory (Gaza 2006). More recent, but apparently equally stable, is the Jordanian-Israeli Peace Agreement of 1994 which has led to lively, surprisingly warm relations at official levels. Even on the Syrian-Israeli front, quiet since the 1974 disengagement of forces agreement, the two countries have been quite close to agreement in the sporadic negotiations that have taken place over the past decade and, therefore, might well reach final success once the international climate allows for resumption of bilateral talks. Thus, the Arab-Israeli conflict might be viewed today as on the way out.

In fact, what has happened is that the conflict between states—as the Arab-Israeli conflict was internationally viewed for many years—has almost drawn to an end. But this has brought matters to the very heart of the conflict, the issue at its very core: Israel and Palestine. The apparently intractable conflict is the one between two peoples, two national movements for self-determination on the same piece of land viewed as homeland by both and perceived as essential to the identification and existence of each.

The sources of the Israeli-Palestinian conflict may be found in the advent of political Zionism, with its dream of self-determination for the Jewish people in their ancient homeland.[1] The Zionist movement was born primarily in response to and as a part of the development of nationalism and national states in Europe—states in which the Jews were a minority, with a national identity of their own. Not long after the rise of nationalism in Europe, the same phenomenon spread in the Middle East; by the early twentieth century, nascent Arab nationalism had emerged, spawning in time Palestinian national identification as well. The two were headed for a clash, and clashes indeed came in the form of riots in the 1920s and the 1930s, as Jewish immigration and land acquisition threatened economic and even political dispossession of the local Palestinian population. Fighting each other, the two peoples (neither of which was regarded as a "people" by the other) ultimately also fought for independence from the British Empire.

The British had been assigned a League of Nations mandate over Palestine[2] when World War I brought an end to the Turkish Empire that had reigned over the region. Shortly thereafter, in 1922, the British ceded the part of the Palestinian mandate east of the Jordan River to Transjordan; the remainder, west of the Jordan River, came to be known as Mandated Palestine. The Mandate affirmed the Balfour declaration of 1917, in which the British had officially promised "to view with favor the establishment in Palestine of a national home for the Jewish people." Although the British had earlier made more ambiguous, contradictory promises to the Hashemite Sharif Hussein bin Ali, Emir of Mecca as well.

These apparently conflicting promises notwithstanding, during the period of the Mandate the British showed few signs of relinquishing the area, either to Jew or Arab, but the growing violence inside the country led them to eventually propose plans for autonomy, partition and even population transfers. In the aftermath of World War II the violence between Jew and Arab had become so strong in Palestine that the British decided, finally, to give up the Mandate. The United Nations, explicitly under the impact of the horrors of the European Holocaust, voted in favor of partitioning Palestine for the creation of a Jewish state and an Arab state. This decision, UN General Assembly Resolution 181 of 29 November 1947 (the Partition Plan), led to Palestinian Arab attacks on Jews and civil war within Palestine. The State of Israel was declared by the Jews on 15 May 1948. No corresponding Arab state was created, primarily because of the absence of a strong local Palestinian leadership but also because of territorial interests of the surrounding Arab states, particularly Transjordan (which had obtained its independence from Britain in 1946 and changed its name to the Hashemite Kingdom of Jordan). With the declaration of the State of Israel, the Arab states (Egypt, Lebanon, Iraq, Syria and Jordan) invaded. The war ended a year and half later with Israel in possession of roughly one-third more land than accorded it by the UN Partition Plan, and some 600,000–700,000 Palestinian refugees who had fled or been expelled by Israel in the course of the hostilities. Jordan captured the West Bank (which was territory that was to have gone to the Arab state according to the Partition Plan) and annexed this area in 1950, a move recognized officially by only two states, Britain and Pakistan. The Partition Plan had also called for Jerusalem to be an international city, but in the fighting Jordan had taken East Jerusalem (including the Old City) and Israel West Jerusalem (declaring it as its capital). Israel signed armistice agreements with Jordan, Syria and Egypt, in some cases with minor exchanges of land or territorial adjustments, creating the de facto borders of Israel (never officially recognized nor ever declared a border by Israel). The armistice lines of 1949, with only minor unofficial changes over the years, are what came to be known after the 1967 war as the 4 June 1967 lines.

For the international community at the time the only "Palestinian" problem was that of the refugees, while the conflict itself, until the end of the 1960s, was viewed primarily as a dispute between Israel and the Arab states, and not as one between two national movements or two peoples. This attitude persisted even after the 1967 war, in the course of which Israel occupied the West Bank, along with the Sinai desert and the Syrian (Golan) Heights.[3] In November 1967, the UN Security Council adopted Resolution 242 calling for Israeli withdrawal from territories occupied in the war but referring to the Palestinian issue not as a matter of national self-determination but rather as a refugee issue, for which a just solution was to be found.

It was basically only after the 1967 war and the entry of Fatah under Yasser Arafat into the Palestine Liberation Organization that the Palestinian issue began to be regarded internationally as a matter of the national liberation of a people. Prior to the war the PLO had been largely under Egyptian control and of little power or significance. Fatah, created in 1964, had been more independent and militant, carrying out raids against Israel from bases in Syria. It was these raids that had in fact led to the escalation that ultimately culminated in the 1967 war. With Arafat's assumption of the PLO leadership in 1969 the organization became better known, primarily because of its attacks both internationally and inside Israel. It gained the backing of the Soviet Union in addition to, and in part because of, support already accorded by the Arab states and others. By the mid-1970s the organization had become a major player in the conflict, recognized by most of the world as the legitimate representative of the Palestinian people, whose right to self-determination was also increasingly recognized.

Israel for its part would have nothing to do with the PLO; nor did it recognize the Palestinians as a people. The matter of the occupied territories was perceived as an issue between Israel and the Arab states, namely Jordan regarding the West Bank, and Egypt regarding Gaza. Thus, the ruling Labor Party in Israel considered returning territory, in exchange for peace, only to the surrounding states. Following the 1967 war, there were various Israeli government decisions to hold onto most of the West Bank and Gaza, while there were also proposals regarding autonomy or partial withdrawals for these territories—within a general policy of "land for peace." Israeli law was extended to East Jerusalem in June 1967, and in 1980, following its ascension to power, a right wing government promulgated a law that officially designated "complete and united" Jerusalem (i.e., east and west Jerusalem together) the capital of Israel. This government, which had ended Labor's virtual monopoly on power in the elections of 1977, abandoned the principle of "land for peace," and in time declared the evacuation of Sinai as having fulfilled the withdrawal requirements of Resolution 242. It also began an extensive settlement project of the West Bank and Gaza so as to prevent any territorial compromise or the emergence of a Palestinian state.[4]

While there were any number of peace plans and proposals suggested over the years, mainly by the Americans and Soviets, but also by Arab states, and there were even direct negotiations briefly in 1973, followed eventually by the Israeli-Egyptian peace agreement in 1979, the Israeli-Palestinian conflict only intensified. But, as Israeli governments moved in an increasingly hawkish direction after 1977, the PLO moved in the opposite direction, particularly following the 1982 Israeli invasion of Lebanon (designed to destroy the Palestinian organization based there). In late 1988, after a year of the Intifada (civilian uprising) within the West Bank and Gaza, the PLO declared an end both to its use of terrorism/armed struggle and its goal of eliminating the state of Israel by accepting the idea of creating a Palestinian state in the West Bank and Gaza, next to rather than instead of the state of Israel. In light of this, under a new government elected in 1992, led by Yitzhak Rabin and the Labor Party, Israel was ready to sit down with the PLO and discuss the possibilities for peace.

▣ Peace Plans

Beginning with the 1993 Oslo Accords and up to the Disengagement of 2005, there were a large number of peace plans and proposals for ending the violence and even resolving the hundred-year old conflict between Israel and the Palestinians in the Land of Israel/Palestine. Historic claims and aspirations, along with borders—official and unofficial—were examined, challenged and in some cases accepted. Frustration and concern, to a large degree from outside the region as well as from inside, produced often quite detailed plans or proposals for entering or returning to the path of peacemaking. And the parties to the conflict, themselves, whether through official or track-two efforts,

tried to come up with solutions to the problems, dealing with the various issues of the conflict, and reaching certain agreements. In time there were those
who even provided a model for a final peace accord. The time and context of
each proposal or agreement varied, and impacted on the final products. The
individuals involved in the formulations along with the parties themselves
had their influence as well—from the President of the United States to the
advisors of the negotiators. None of the proposals was haphazard or frivo-
lous, though some reflected the deep mistrust between the parties along with
the fears and growing skepticism within the two societies—born not only of
historic experience but also from the disappointments and violence of the
period. Indeed the greatest challenge was to fathom a way to cope with these
factors and to find responses that might "work." Unfair, imposed or unrealistic proposals would not provide genuine or lasting solutions. There was the
question as to whether a "just" solution would even be possible, given the
inherent contradiction between what constituted justice in the eyes of each of
the parties, with their national, historic and sometimes spiritual claims to the
same piece of land. "Conflicting narratives," as this came to be called, pervad-
ed the discussions, with all their emotional and psychological legacies. Finally,
there was the question as to whether any solution was even possible. Terms
such as "conflict management" rather than "conflict resolution," "ripeness,"
that is, the absence of readiness for agreement on the part of the two peoples,
"intractability" of the differences and issues, reflected growing pessimism as
the peace process began to break down.

This process itself is of undoubted interest, and fascinating personal accounts have been written by many of the participants and observers.[5] Some
relate to the no less important cultural, linguistic or tactical problems that
characterized the process. From these varied accounts, however, and the pub-
licity surrounding the process, it is often difficult to fathom exactly what each
proposal in fact envisaged substantively for solution of the conflict. It is my
intention, therefore, to examine the main points of each plan or proposal
as they relate to the major issues of the conflict (borders, security, refugees,
Jerusalem), the evolution or refinement of the suggested solutions, along
with various ideas for bridging the gaps or plans for moving into and through

negotiations. The problems and pitfalls inherent in various proposals, along with the reactions to them, are also analyzed, all with the purpose of determining just where matters were left on each issue, at the official and unofficial level, pending a possible resumption of negotiations.

CHAPTER TWO

The Oslo Accords, 1993–1999

▣ Toward Oslo

The road to Oslo was a long one for both Israelis and Palestinians. For each it was a matter of a very gradual change in thinking marked by bitter internal dispute, outside pressures, and the tragic experience of loss and bloodshed over many decades. For both, in many ways, the Palestinian Intifada that began in December 1987 was the decisive event that led to Oslo. Many other factors and events, both before and after, played significant roles, but the Intifada may have tipped the scales in favor of the direction that finally brought about the Oslo Accords.

For the Palestinians the process that brought them to Oslo could be traced as far back as the early 1970s when a debate was opened within the PLO over the future status of areas of Palestine that would be liberated and a possible relationship with Israel. The idea of creating a Palestinian state limited to the West Bank and Gaza, a "mini-state" next to, rather than instead of, the state of Israel, namely the two-state solution, was proposed by some (including the PLO's backers in Moscow[1]). After the PLO's serious setback

9

as a result of Israel's invasion of Lebanon in 1982, this became a heated and bloody debate within the organization, with some advocates for recognizing Israel and the two-state solution, such as Sa'id Hamami and Issam Sartawi, assassinated for pursuing these views. The Lebanon War had led to a serious rift within the PLO, a takeover attempt by Syria and a challenge to Arafat's authority by militant elements within his own Fatah. Yet, at the same time, the war persuaded many others that Palestinian armed struggle was no match for the Israeli military machine and that moreover neither the Arab states nor the Soviet Union was willing to go to war for them. Indeed by 1988 Gorbachev was in power in the Soviet Union with an entirely new "balanced" policy regarding the Arab-Israeli conflict—edging toward renewed relations with Israel and urging Arafat to do the same.[2]

Arafat himself was apparently moving in this direction as evidenced by his attempted rapprochement with Jordan and his overtures to the United States in late 1984 and early 1985.[3] The United States demanded PLO acceptance of UNSC Resolution 242 and explicit recognition of Israel's right to exist, along with renunciation of terror, as conditions for opening any US-PLO dialogue. The outbreak of the Intifada constituted pressure from below, demonstrating the untenable situation of the Palestinians under occupation and demanding a breakthrough. These circumstances, then, of disillusionment with outside (Arab and Soviet) assistance and frustration and despair from inside the occupied territories, brought the PLO's long debate to its culmination and denouement in the form of the political resolution of the Palestine National Council in November 1988 accepting Resolution 242 and condemning terrorism, followed by an Arafat speech to the UNGA and press conference in Geneva explicitly recognizing Israel's right to exist in peace and security and renouncing all forms or terrorism.[4] In doing this the PLO adopted the two-state solution in what it called its "historic compromise" to accept a state in only part (twenty-two percent) of Mandated Palestine (Mandated Palestine being the area between the Jordan River and the Mediterranean Sea). Politically the PLO was now ready for a peace process. Further deterioration in its strength, with the final loss of the PLO's political backer, the Soviet Union, and perhaps still more importantly the loss of its main financial backer, Saudi

Arabia, due to Arafat's pro-Iraq position in the 1990–1991 Gulf crisis, were added to the continued pressure from inside the territories. Thus it would appear that pragmatic considerations, isolation and perhaps the understanding that the only other alternative was continued occupation, brought the PLO to Oslo.

It took Israel a bit longer to reach the point of readiness in recognizing the PLO and a compromise solution. Israeli society had long been divided over the future of the occupied territories. Labor Party governments advocated "land for peace" but explicitly rejected both the PLO and the idea of a Palestinian state, while right-wing governments sought to maintain and place settlers in the occupied territories, especially the West Bank, often for religious as well as nationalist reasons. Yet opinion polls and surveys over the years from 1967 to the early 1990s indicated a gradual shift in public opinion in the direction of a willingness to compromise over the territories and even, albeit to a far lesser degree, to accept of the idea of a Palestinian state. A graph of public opinion indicated a gradual trend with a sharp "jump" in this direction at the time of the Intifada. Whereas prior to the outbreak of the Intifada a majority of Israelis preferred the "status quo" with regard to the territories, this percentage was to drop significantly.[5] For many Israelis the Intifada led to the realization that there was actually no such thing as a "status quo," but rather the situation was dynamic. And, moreover, the direction it was taking might not be in Israel's favor. Put in other words, the argument that many of the Israeli left had been making for some time now gained greater credence: one could not maintain an occupation and deny rights to a people—by this time over three million Palestinians—and expect them to accept the situation quietly, and indefinitely. Thus, rather than enhancing Israel's security, the territories were now a threat to one's personal security. And with the growing trend toward consumerism and individualism in Israeli society, a certain war-weariness could be detected, a desire to get on with one's life, without the risks and threats that came with holding on to the territories. Opinion polls did not indicate a basic change in the public's attitude toward the Palestinians; there was not an ideological shift toward understanding or accepting Palestinian demands. On the contrary, fear and hostility regarding the Palestinians increased during the Intifada. But pragmatism and self-interest were seen to dictate compromise in the interest of bringing the conflict to a close.

It was in part this change in public opinion that brought Yitzhak Rabin and the Labor Party back to power in the 1992 elections, paving the way to Oslo. In his own path to Oslo, Rabin may have been motivated by more than public opinion. While Rabin had first preferred peace with Syria, as a military man having always considered Arab states a greater existential threat to Israel than the PLO, he was willing, albeit skeptical, to pursue any track that might bring about a settlement. Rabin believed that the situation was ripe for progress; he spoke of a "window of opportunity." This window was the result of the changes taking place in the world: the collapse of the Soviet Union and the emergence of the United States as the sole superpower, the "new world order." The United States in the wake of the Gulf War, and in part as a result of Arab participation in the anti-Iraq coalition, sought regional stability undisturbed by the Arab-Israeli conflict. (This in fact had brought about earlier pressure on Israel to agree to the relatively futile Madrid Conference of 1991.[6]) At the same time, the Arab states now had to look to the US, both politically and economically, and also counter the growing domestic threats to their regimes from extremist Islam. According to Rabin, the Arab world was divided and weak, as was the PLO in the wake of the Gulf War, while Iran, on the other hand, under its Islamic leadership was developing a nuclear capability (already known to Israel at the time). Given his concern over the spread of weapons of mass destruction in the region, Rabin wanted to take the Arab-Israeli conflict, specifically Israel, out of this equation, while the circumstances in the world and the region at this time seemed most auspicious for a breakthrough.

▪ The Accords

"Oslo" was actually a series of agreements, all within the overall category of "Interim Arrangements" for the West Bank and Gaza Strip until the conclusion of an agreement on the final status of these territories. As we shall see, it may have been the very "interim" nature of these agreements that led to their downfall. The underlying concept was that the two sides were not yet ready for a full peace agreement, and therefore, an interim period was needed during which to build mutual trust. However, this basic concept was fraught with a number of problems: one, an illusion that peace had been reached, with an accompanying expectation of changes on the ground—when in fact peace had not yet been negotiated and therefore reality on the ground could not live up to expectations;[7] two, having left the final status of the territories for future negotiations meant that the goal was undefined, a matter of particular importance for the Palestinians for there was no mention of what the end result would be for them; and three, although the interim period was to be limited in time, to five years, this provided a relatively extended period for opponents to a final settlement to disrupt the entire process and bring it to a close. Thus, trust, which one might expect to be the result of a peace agreement and a period of reconciliation, was made a pre-condition for such an agreement—a basic flaw in conceptualization that preceded both omissions and mistakes within the interim agreements themselves and the problems in implementation.

The following are the agreements that made up what is known as "The Oslo Accords":

- Letters of Mutual Recognition between Israel and the PLO—
  9,10 September 1993
- Declaration of Principles on Interim Self-Government Arrangement
  ("Oslo I")—13 September 1993
- [Paris] Protocol on Economic Relations—29 April 1994
- Agreement on Gaza Strip and the Jericho Area ("Cairo Agreement")—
  4 May 1994
- Agreement on Preparatory Transfer of Powers and Responsibilities—
  29 August 1994 (additional agreement 28 August 1995)
- Israeli-Palestinian Interim Agreement on the West Bank and the Gaza
  Strip ("Oslo II")—28 September 1995

- Protocol Concerning the Redeployment in Hebron—15 January 1996
- Wye River Memorandum—23 October 1998
- Sharm el-Sheikh Memorandum—4 September 1999

The Letters of Mutual Recognition were in many ways the most important of all the documents because they represented the historic breakthrough and constituted perhaps the only irreversible move in the whole process: mutual recognition.

Yasser Arafat's letter to Rabin expressed, before all else, the PLO's recognition of "the right of Israel to exist in peace and security." Thus it not only acknowledged the fact of Israel's existence but also asserted Israel's right to exist, its legitimacy, unchallenged by threat or war. This is basically what Sadat had offered in 1977 and what Israel had sought from its Arab neighbors from the earliest days of the state. This acknowledgement also meant, of course, that the PLO abandoned its goal of eliminating the state of Israel—explicitly stated in the letter's commitment to remove from the PLO Charter all articles that denied Israel's right to exist or were inconsistent with these commitments. Further, the PLO explicitly renounced the use of terror and all forms of violence, even though this was already implied in the right of Israel to exist in peace and security. The letter also carried the PLO's acceptance of Resolution 242 which contained not only the right of all states in the region, including Israel, to recognized and secure borders, but also laid down at least the outer limits of territories to be evacuated by Israel, namely, territories occupied in 1967.[8] In other words, in accepting Resolution 242 the PLO was limiting whatever aspirations it had to no more than the territory lost in 1967.

Yitzhak Rabin's letter to Arafat came in response to these commitments. In fewer words and with fewer commitments, but no less significantly, the Israeli Prime Minister presented the government decision to "recognize the PLO as the representative of the Palestinian people." Thus, Israel acknowledged the Palestinians as a nation. No longer could Israel claim that there was no such thing as a Palestinian people; they were a nation, with a national movement. No longer could Israel try to find quislings in the occupied territories with whom to deal—the only representative was now the PLO.[9] Also, Israel could no longer pretend that the Palestinian problem was one solely of refugees (as referred to in Resolution 242)—a specific if difficult issue—but rather, a people and as such possessing basic rights such as the right of a people to freedom and self-determination even if this was not stated explicitly.

Unlike Arafat, Rabin made no commitments in the letter beyond recognition. This presumably was a reflection of the asymmetry and weakened position of the PLO, a liberation movement facing a state—and a state that had full backing from the only superpower, one that had already in the past dictated the only terms acceptable to Israel for dealing with the PLO.[10] Indeed the additional commitments in Arafat's letter were of a more temporal nature—they could be and in some cases were reversed. Recognition of a right, however, was not a revocable measure even if implementation were subject to debate or challenge at a later time. Mutual recognition was the minimum requirement for the opening of the peace process.

Oslo I was far from a peace agreement but rather a **"Declaration of Principles"** (DOP), a framework[11] or blueprint as it were, for temporary arrangements by which the territories were to be administered pending the determination of their final status. The title contained the words "Self-Government Arrangements," reminiscent of the various plans for Palestinian autonomy that had been raised by Israel in the past. Indeed the DOP greatly resembled the autonomy plan proposed by Menachem Begin in the Camp David talks with Egypt in 1978 and in some ways also the 1969 Rogers Plan. Indeed, the DOP was a guideline for autonomy, even relatively limited autonomy. This is not to belittle or deny the importance of the DOP. It provided for significant precedent-setting and empowering steps, and it did in fact contain many extremely important clauses meant to direct and impact upon the final status.

In a preamble that was to be repeated in virtually all the subsequent agreements, the DOP reiterated the recognition contained in the letters. However, the formulation was phrased somewhat differently: the two sides agreed "to put an end to decades of confrontation and conflict, recognize their mutual legitimate and political rights, and strive to live in peaceful coexistence and mutual dignity and security and achieve a just, lasting and comprehensive peace settlement and historic reconciliation." Years of indirect and secret talks, track-two and citizen diplomacy, draft proposals and peace plans all lay behind each word and expression, including that which was not said. The new, somewhat ambiguous recognition of the two sides' "mutual legitimate and political rights" seemed to be an effort to avoid the term "national rights." This was most likely because of Israeli reluctance to even imply national independence (statehood) for the Palestinians at that time, although a just, lasting and comprehensive peace settlement was identified as the goal. The word "just" is no less ambiguous but often demanded by the Palestinians, who view themselves as the historically "wronged party" in the conflict, especially in connection with the refugee problem; it is also coupled with their interest in living in "mutual dignity" after years of occupation. Israel's interests are expressed in the "end of conflict" and a "lasting" peace along with living in "security" parts of the formula. "Comprehensive" is a term Israel had tried to avoid in the past since this could imply peace with all the other parties to the conflict as a condition for peace with any one party to the conflict through bilateral talks. Yet it can also mean merely all the issues involved in the bilateral peace and therefore acceptable, albeit with reluctance, by Israel. Clearly everything depended upon interpretation, as was classically the case with Resolution 242—the cornerstone upon which all Arab-Israeli proposals and agreements had to be based.

The first article of the DOP stipulated that the interim arrangements were for a limited transition period of five years. Transition to what was not stated inasmuch as that was to be determined by the final status talks. But the time limit of five years, with negotiations on the final status to begin no later than three years from the beginning of the transition was the most important point. Whatever the final status turned out to be, Israel would not be permitted to drag out either negotiations or the interim period indefinitely as various leaders and parties in Israel had sought in the past, and presumably would continue to seek in the future. Yet there was no guarantee that the final status would in fact be a total end to Israeli rule over the West Bank and Gaza. Nor, of course, was there any guarantee that the final status would meet all of Israel's demands, although the asymmetry of the two sides placed Israel in a better position.

The timetable was for a gradual transfer of power from Israel to the Palestinians in four stages. The whole "Oslo process" would begin only with stage one, in which governing powers would be transferred in the Gaza Strip and Jericho. This was to be accomplished over no more than a six-month period. Israel had preferred to begin with Gaza alone, but the Palestinians, fearing a division and possible loss of continuation of the process on the West Bank, insisted upon Jericho as well at this stage. Stage two, to follow immediately, would be transfer of some civil authority (e.g., education, health, welfare, tourism, local taxes, etc.) to the Palestinians throughout the entire West Bank. In stage three a formal interim agreement would be negotiated for implementation of the DOP, including delineation of the powers of a self-governing Palestinian authority and elected council, election procedures and similar measures. All of these stages were to be completed in nine months from the beginning of withdrawal from Gaza and Jericho. Stage four, final status negotiations, was to begin "as soon as possible," but no later than the beginning of the third year—which came to be May 1996, three years after the actual withdrawal from Gaza and Jericho. These negotiations were to deal with the issues of refugees, settlements, security, borders, water, and Jerusalem.

Aside from the timetable and many clauses regarding procedures during the interim period, such as elections, services, public order, and liaison, the DOP laid down certain guiding principles of lasting importance. The three most important of these were as follows.

1) Nothing done or agreed upon during the interim period was to prejudice or pre-empt the outcome of the final status negotiations (Article V–4).

> While not spelled out, this could mean, and probably was interpreted by the Palestinians to mean, that lands expropriated, Jewish settlements expanded or created, areas that continued to be held by Israel and other such measures would not be binding or permanent. Since the Palestinians had been unable to get anything into the DOP regarding a freeze on settlement building (the Israeli negotiators claimed there was no need for this since the ruling Labor Party had already introduced a freeze on new settlements),[12] this clause became most important to counter Israeli settlement activity.

2) The area referred to, specifically the jurisdiction of the elected Palestinian authority, with certain exceptions left for final status, was to be the West Bank and Gaza Strip which were to be viewed as "a single territorial unit, whose integrity will be preserved during the interim period" (Article IV).

> This clause was meant to prevent a separation of the two areas politically or economically, but also to prevent Israeli annexations or expropriations by means of road building, settlements or other measures. It reflected the Palestinians insistence that their willingness to abandon their earlier goals of all of Palestine did not mean that they would now negotiate over the borders of the part left to them, the West Bank and Gaza or, as generally expressed, their demand for total Israeli withdrawal to the 4 June 1967 lines. Israel for its part was unwilling to make a commitment to this border (the "green line"), adhering to the Israeli Foreign Ministry interpretation that the West Bank was "disputed territory" and that Resolution 242 did not necessitate withdrawal from "all" the territories, i.e., all of the West Bank.

3) Disputes with regard to interpretation or implementation of the DOP and subsequent agreements during the interim period were to be resolved through negotiations via an Israeli-Palestinian liaison committee or by means of arbitration or other agreed means (Articles X, XV).

> This was interpreted later as a commitment to refrain from the use of force or violence, evoked particularly by Israel when violence broke out (the Al-Aksa Intifada) in 2000. It was not clear if arbitration was to be conducted by a third party. No third party was actually called for in the DOP, although the Protocol on Israeli withdrawal from the Gaza Strip and Jericho (Appendix II) allowed for a "temporary international or foreign presence, as agreed upon." Actually one of the flaws of the Oslo Accords, as we shall see below, is that they did not provide for third party observer or peacekeeping involvement.

These three basic principles—reiterated in almost all of the subsequent Oslo agreements—were designed not only to govern the interim period but also to preserve conditions conducive to fair final status negotiations. In a sense these principles were meant as assurances to both sides that neither side would try to take advantage of the period in question in order to improve its own position or harm that of the other side. As such they illustrated the lack of trust, indeed the high degree of mistrust, existing between the two parties at the time. Other important but more specific clauses, such as security, Israeli redeployments, and safe passage, will be dealt with below.

The Paris Protocol, negotiated once the withdrawal from Gaza and Jericho began in late April 1994, was a detailed document designed to regulate economic relations between Israel and the Palestinians as well as between the Gaza Strip and the West Bank. While it did not provide for economic union, it established understandings for a limited customs union, transfer of goods, taxes, and monetary relations. It also included a provision for monthly transfer of revenues by Israel to the PA from various direct and indirect taxes (such as VAT, petrol tax, and taxes for health and social security) collected by Israel which amounted to approximately sixty percent of the Palestinian yearly budget. The Paris Protocol remained in effect, although not fully implemented (specifically in the area of revenue transfers), and was later called into question by Israel with regard to post-disengagement Gaza.

The two subsequent agreements, the **Gaza Strip-Jericho Area Agreement** of 4 May 1994 and the **Preparatory Transfer of Powers and Responsibilities** of 29 August 1994 had not been especially called for in the DOP and may not, legally, have been necessary. They were primarily the result of repeated delays, disputes and haggling over implementation procedures, necessitating far more detailed attention to the measures introduced in this interim period, including the Palestinian institutions, security matters, safe passage, and specific issues which had arisen such as missing persons and the details of the actual transfer of powers from the Israeli civil administration to the Palestinians. The scheduled withdrawal from Jericho and the Gaza Strip, which was to signal the commencement of the timetable, had not yet begun, and therefore the Gaza-Jericho Agreement called for an accelerated withdrawal within three weeks. Illustrative of the disputes and mutual suspicions that had been growing in the preceding months, the signing ceremony of the Gaza-Jericho Agreement in Cairo was temporarily disrupted when Arafat questioned the map indicating the area of Jericho from which Israel would withdraw. A new element introduced in the Gaza-Jericho Agreement was a clause regarding "prevention of hostile acts," prompted, at least in part, by terrorist attacks conducted by Hamas and the Islamic Jihad which had begun almost immediately after the signing of the DOP. This clause also stipulated protection of settlers and Palestinians from mutual attacks, which had also been taking place.

Confidence-building measures were added to the Gaza-Jericho Agreement in the form of promised prisoner releases. Israel agreed to release about five thousand Palestinian prisoners within a five-week period and to negotiate further prisoner releases. Moreover, Israel agreed to permit Palestinians to return from abroad to the Gaza Strip or the West Bank and not subject them to prosecution for offenses committed prior to the DOP (13 September 1993). For their part, the Palestinians were to solve the problem of persons who had cooperated with Israeli authorities in the past. This was due to a spate of Palestinian killings of persons accused of collaboration. A potentially significant innovation of the Gaza-Jericho Agreement was the provision for the deployment of a Temporary International Presence (TIP) of 400 persons from five or six donor countries for a six-month period. While the TIP was to consist of "observers, instructors and other experts," its role and authority were to be negotiated by Israel and the Palestinian Authority (PA).

After over two years from the signing of the DOP, the **Interim Agreement on the West Bank and the Gaza Strip (Oslo II)** was finally signed on 28 September 1995. It embodied all of the clauses in the DOP and measures governing the creation of the Palestinian Authority, elections to the Palestinian Council, safe passage between Gaza and the West Bank, air and seaports for Gaza, as well as repeating the basic principles or DOP, which were also included in all the previous agreements. The Interim Agreement also provided for measures covered but not yet implemented by previous agreements such as the prisoner releases, the issue of collaborators and control of violence, and the abrogation of parts of the PLO charter as promised in Arafat's letter to Rabin.

Apparently in response to the continued building of new settlements and the expansion of existing ones, a principle was added barring either side from "any step that will change the status of the West Bank and Gaza Strip" pending the outcome of final statusnegotiations. This article (XXXI) was added to the principle that nothing in the agreement would prejudice or pre-empt the outcome of the final status talks. These two articles, now encoded in the Interim Agreement, became the basis for Palestinian charges against settlement construction, despite the absence of specific mention of settlement construction in any of the agreements.

The major innovation of the Interim Agreement was the new timetable, which spelled out the redeployments for the Israeli army and the division of authority between Israel and the Palestinians. (The term "redeployment" rather than "withdrawal" was now used, presumably to provide greater flexibility for Israel[13]). In the first stage of redeployments, Israel would withdraw from the remaining populated areas (Jericho and Gaza having been evacuated), namely the six cities on the West Bank, leaving the seventh, Hebron, for some months later. Three subsequent redeployments were to take place at six-month intervals over a period of eighteen months. The areas evacuated would be divided into: area A—to be under full Palestinian control (the cities); area B—Palestinian civil responsibility, Israeli security responsibility; and area C—full Israeli control. Areas A and B were expected to contain the vast majority of the Palestinian population

The Interim Agreement, as the basic document for the interim period, also codified the provisions regarding not only the redeployments but also Jerusalem, settlements, security and, as noted, the Palestinian PLO Charter.

How Jerusalem, specifically East Jerusalem, was to be handled had long been a problem. The Palestinians viewed Jerusalem (that part of the city that had been under Jordan prior to the 1967 war) as part of the West Bank and the political, civic, social and cultural center of the area. Israel, which had annexed the eastern part of Jerusalem (1967) and legislated its status as the unified capital of Israel (1980), refused even to discuss the status of city. In view of this, the Palestinians agreed that Jerusalem would be dealt with separately from the rest of the West Bank in the final status negotiations, and the

Oslo II Redeployments (1998 to present)

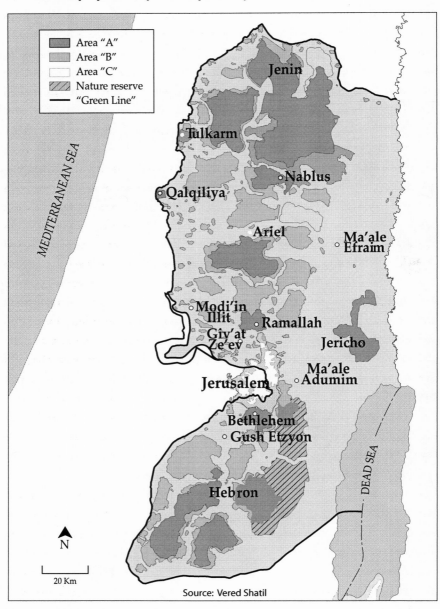

Source: Vered Shatil

Transfer of Powers agreement specifically excluded Jerusalem from the jurisdiction of the West Bank. Both sides agreed to a mention of the holy sites as
open to all. Most importantly, the Palestinians insisted on a clause permitting
East Jerusalemites to vote for the Palestinian Council. Israel was unwilling to
have this concession publicized so the clause was included only in an annex
to Oslo I. Nonetheless, it appeared in the body of the text of Oslo II-The
Interim Agreement.

While there was a timetable for withdrawal of Israeli forces and stipulations about control in the three areas, the exact points to which Israel would
withdraw were far from clear. The Interim Agreement, like all the Oslo documents before it, stipulated that the West Bank and Gaza Strip constituted one
territorial unit (with the exclusion of Jerusalem as noted above), but the lines
had yet to be drawn within these areas. For example, during the withdrawal
from the Gaza Strip, the Israeli military was evacuated but the settlements and
Israeli settlers remained. Moreover, Israel was to retain free use of the roads
by its military and civilians along with the responsibility for external security
around the areas evacuated in the Gaza Strip and also Jericho. With the next
redeployment from the populated areas, withdrawal to "specified military locations" and the delineation of the three subsequent redeployments was to be
determined with each redeployment. The final lines were to be negotiated in
the final status talks. Though not stated, and contested by the Palestinians,
Israel maintained that it alone would decide the scope of each of the required
redeployments before the final status talks. In the course of the redeployments, parts of area B were to become area A, parts of area C were to become
area B and eventually area A, but no specifications were provided as to which
parts of each area were to be affected.

As opposed to what was probably intentional ambiguity regarding the
withdrawals, provisions for security were detailed and exhaustive—in part
covered in the voluminous annexes to the Agreement. Israel was to maintain
all external security, which included not only border areas but also the borders or edges of area A, namely entrances and exits to the Palestinian cities.
In addition, Israel was to provide security for all the settlements and settlers
in all the areas and over-all security in areas B and C, although there would
be Palestinian police in area B. There were complicated regulations regard-

ing the movement of Palestinian police and joint Israeli-Palestinian patrols, with the Palestinians permitted a "strong" police force consisting of 12,000 in the West Bank and 18,000 in the Gaza Strip. The amounts and types of their equipment and weapons were specified in the Agreement. The Palestinians were responsible for combating terrorism, with a set of complicated rules that involved trying suspected terrorists or turning them over to Israel.

Oslo I and II were very well received by both publics, with roughly 65 percent support in each society remaining constant for the first few years. Popular enthusiasm and optimism were evidenced by a rush to open contacts and the creation of tens if not hundreds of joint projects at the grassroots level, from joint kindergartens to joint business ventures, often initiated by recently released Palestinian prisoners whose knowledge of Hebrew and status as heroes in their society put them in good standing. Opponents were also evident, with opposition groups within the PLO as well as outside it. The PFLP and the DFLP, while supporting a peace process with Israel, opposed the Oslo Accords because of the absence of any promise or even mention of statehood. From their point of view, Israel offered only autonomy, thereby freeing itself of the economic burden of the Palestinian population while granting itself overall control and keeping its settlements. The Islamist groups rejected the peace process altogether and violently opposed Oslo, unleashing increasingly intrusive terrorism to stop the peace process. On the Israeli side, opposition came from the right-wing parties and all of the religious parties in time. The vote in the Knesset had only a majority of one in favor (61), with 50 opposed (including Ariel Sharon), 8 abstentions (including Ehud Barak, then a Labor minister) and 1 absent. The settlers were the most vehement and occasionally violent opponents, focusing their campaign on Rabin, whom they dubbed a traitor.

From the start, implementation of the agreements was repeatedly delayed, with disputes over a large number of issues such as voting in East Jerusalem, the size of Jericho, the powers of the Palestinian Authority and Council, safe passage—all at the beginning of the process—and later, issues such as the growing violence, the PLO Charter, the redeployments and border crossings.[14] As a result, it took seven rather than two months to implement the first step which was the withdrawal from Jericho and the Gaza Strip, and another four months to reach the formal transfer of civil powers to the Palestinians and another year to get the formal Interim Agreement. Even the implementation of the Interim Agreement's first redeployment was delayed over two months. From an historic perspective, these are not long periods, but at the time the delays were perceived as reneging on the agreement by one side or the other if not signs of actual deception.

Israel for its part failed to provide the safe passage promised for goods and people between the Gaza Strip and the West Bank; it failed to release anywhere near the numbers of prisoners to which it had agreed; it repeatedly postponed discussions, and most seriously, perhaps, it continued to build and expand settlements, expropriating land for this purpose and for the paving of by-pass roads for the settlers. In addition, when redeployments did take place, Israeli "external security" led to the creation of roadblocks and checkpoints within the territories so that, coupled with a closing of access to East Jerusalem (access was subject to permits), Palestinians found themselves with less rather than more freedom of movement than prior to Oslo. And more of the land of the West Bank and East Jerusalem had disappeared into Israeli hands. Settler violence was also a problem, although the most serious of such incidents, the killing of twenty-nine Muslim worshippers in the Hebron mosque by the settler Baruch Goldstein, was a relatively isolated albeit horrific act of Jewish terrorism.

There were violations of the agreements by the Palestinians as well, including larger numbers of police and weapons than permitted, failure to extradite suspected terrorists, and failure to alter the PLO Charter. The most serious problem emanating from the Palestinians was the increase in terror attacks inside Israel as well as in the territories. Though perpetrated by non-PLO Islamists (Hamas and the Islamic Jihad groups), Arafat and the Palestinian authorities were blamed by Israel for laxity (though not actual complicity) regarding the failure to prevent or deal with the growing terrorism. In retrospective comparison with the violence of the 2000–2004 period, the terrorism of the Oslo period was relatively limited to an average of one attack per month. But in the context of the time, these mainly suicide bombings of civilians were far more frequent and far more traumatic than anything experienced in the past. Therefore they strengthened the opponents of the peace process among the Israeli public, egged on the extremists among them, and whittled away popular support for Oslo.

Extremist hysteria finally erupted into the assassination of Rabin by Yigal Amir, a religious, Jewish student, at the end of a massive peace rally in Tel Aviv in support of Oslo on 4 November 1995—just two months after the signing of the Interim Agreement.

Only after the shock of Rabin's assassination did Israel begin the first redeployment called for in the Interim Agreement. Over the next two months Israel withdrew from all the Palestinian cities with the exception of Hebron. These withdrawals made it possible to hold the delayed elections for the Palestinian Legislative Council in January 1996 (withdrawal from most of Hebron was supposed to take place twenty-two days before the elections, but was postponed). However, the positive effect of the withdrawals and elections was totally destroyed by a wave of terrorist attacks in Israeli cities that killed some 64 people within a little over one week from 25 February to 4 March 1996. The attacks were said to have been in retaliation for the Israeli killing of a leading Palestinian terror suspect, but that did not in any way minimize their impact, virtually bringing the peace process to a halt. The terrorist attacks also came to a near total halt, but the fact that Arafat now, so belatedly, cracked down on the terrorists (and finally had the PNC abrogate the offensive clauses in the PLO charter[15]), only served to strengthen the impression that the Palestinian leader could have acted before, had he wanted to. Although the terrorism had been designed (like the assassination of Rabin by a right-wing Israeli) to stop the peace process, in fact a cycle had set in by 1994—one that was to repeat itself far more intensely later, in post-Oslo years. Acts of terror had bred Israeli reprisals and delays in implementation of the peace process; these in turn had led to still further terrorism, and then reprisals, and so on. The result was indeed the end of the peace process, with the return of the right wing to power in Israel and the election of Benyamin Netanyahu in May 1996. The assassination of Rabin played a critical role as well, for Rabin might have weathered the devastating terrorist attacks of 1996 given his security credentials in the eyes of the public. His replacement, Shimon Peres, did not have this advantage.

The Oslo process did not officially end with the election of Netanyahu, but there was no commitment to continue it and there was a declared intention of expanding settlements while explicitly ruling out the possibility of a Palestinian state or negotiations on Jerusalem. Tensions rose as the peace process stalled and settlement activity grew. They erupted in the fall of 1996 when Israel opened a tunnel under the Temple Mount (Haram al-Sharif) theoretically to provide better access to Jewish archeological sites. This was a move that had been avoided by Rabin because of the potentially explosive nature of what was certain to be viewed by the Palestinians as a physical threat to the Muslim holy places above.[16] Palestinian violence did indeed break out in three days of riots throughout the West Bank and Gaza Strip, put down by the Israeli military. Some seventy Palestinians and fifteen Israelis were killed. In response to the violence, President Clinton invited Arafat and Netanyahu to Washington for talks that eventually produced a resumption of Israel's redeployments in the form of the Hebron Protocol.

The Hebron Protocol was intended by Netanyahu merely to revise the previously agreed-upon details for the Israeli withdrawal from eighty percent of the city. However, Arafat insisted, with some support from the Americans, that the Protocol deal with and constitute a part of the Oslo process, including a return to the timetable. As a result of direct intervention by King Hussein of Jordan, the Protocol was signed on 17 January 1997. This was just four months before the total redeployments were to have been completed and the final status talks begun—a deadline that clearly was going to be missed. The Protocol was largely technical, as Netanyahu had sought, dealing with arrangements within and around the city of Hebron. It did have the notable injection of an international "presence," namely the TIP promised in the Interim Agreement, relabeled Temporary International Presence in Hebron (TIPH). Ultimately manned mainly by the Norwegians, TIPH was and remains the only international force ever permitted by Israel inside the occupied territories.[17]

The precedent-setting significance of the Hebron Protocol lay in the fact that it was the first time a right-wing government of Israel agreed to relinquish land, still more significant because this was land in the heart of what was considered Eretz Israel, the Land of Israel, in a city that held religious as well as historic importance for many Jews. Politically, the Protocol was significant for the "Note for the Record" that was attached to it, the result of Arafat's insistence. The Note was the link to the Oslo Accords, committing Netanyahu to continue the process. It delineated the tasks left to the two parties for implementation of the Interim Agreement, along with a new time-table. Netanyahu's innovation was the addition of the phrase "on the basis of reciprocity" which he was to use in the future to make Israeli implementation conditional upon various steps demanded of the Palestinians. This interpreta-tion was used despite the fact that the Note itself said that the commitments of the two sides were to be dealt with "immediately and in parallel."

Once again Israel committed itself to carry out the redeployments, re-lease prisoners, provide the safe-passage between the Gaza Strip and the West Bank, permit the creation of the Gaza airport and seaport, and other specific issues. The Palestinians committed themselves to fight terror, including a list of measures such as "effectively" combating the terrorist "infrastructure," preventing incitement, extraditing suspected terrorists, and confiscating il-legal weapons, along with a commitment to correct the size of the police and the activities and location of governmental offices—a reference presumably to the exclusion of East Jerusalem from Palestinian jurisdiction. There was also a commitment to complete the process of changing the PLO Charter. In April 1996, the PLO had implemented its commitment to abrogate the clauses denying Israel's right to exist, an act acknowledged as such by the Israeli government at the time (Prime Minister Peres).[18] However, the PLO had not codified these changes in a new charter. Although there had been no explicit obligation to produce a new charter, the Netanyahu government now argued that the commitment would not be met until a new charter was writ-ten and enacted.

Finally, the Note presented a new timetable for the redeployments ac-cording to which the eighteen-month period of three redeployments was to begin in March 1997, theoretically ending mid-1998. The 4 May 1997 dead-line for the beginning of final status talks was ignored although the Note said the final status talks "would be resumed" (they had never begun) after imple-mentation of the Hebron Protocol, namely 27 January 1997. In fact, the May

1997 date came and went with no final status talks and virtually no progress following the Hebron Protocol.

The Wye River Memorandum was the result of the stalemate on the ground. Although Israel immediately implemented the withdrawal from roughly eighty percent of Hebron, it neither undertook any of the scheduled redeployments nor met its other commitments regarding prisoners, safe passage, ports, etc. It continued to expand settlement building in the West Bank, especially around and in East Jerusalem. Netanyahu's excuse for non-implementation was primarily the failure of the Palestinians to dismantle the terrorist infrastructure although in fact there were far fewer terrorist attacks in this period than during the Rabin-Peres government. The United States brought pressure on Israel to initiate at least one of the redeployments, even if limited in size. At the same time, Arafat began to threaten unilaterally to declare an independent Palestinian State on 4 May 1999, the date the interim period was to close and the final status was supposed to have been determined. The consequences of such a declaration could only be guessed, but one possible, even probable result might have been Israeli reoccupation of the areas evacuated. In order to avoid a declaration of a Palestinian state, the Wye Memorandum (obtained once again with the direct intervention of the now terminally ill King of Jordan) was intended to restart the Oslo process. It provided a series of renewed commitments including the three long-awaited Israeli "further redeployments" called for in the Interim Agreement subsequent to the withdrawal from the cities. According to the Memorandum, Israel agreed to divide the three remaining redeployments into two phases. Thus the first two redeployments would be combined into one phase, though executed in three stages. The language was convoluted but the important point was that there would now be only two redeployments, the second one to be "addressed by a committee" at some unspecified time. The redeployment that Israel was to undertake two weeks after the Memorandum went into effect, would consist of only thirteen percent of the land of the West Bank, including three percentthat the Palestinians were committed to preserve as "green areas/nature reserves." Thus the breakdown would be one percent to area A and twelve percent to area B, from which the green areas would be closed off. At the same time part of area B (14.2% of it) would become area A. In all, though not mentioned in the Memorandum, the Palestinians would find themselves in control of roughly seventeen percent of the West Bank.[19] Netanyahu stated that the last (future) redeployment would be no more than one percent— yet this was not included in the Memorandum.[20] When viewed together with previous redeployments, had Israel implemented the Wye Memorandum, the Palestinians would have been in full control of 17.1% of the West Bank, partial (civil) control over another 21.8%, with Israel maintaining 61.1%

The Wye Memorandum once again called for all the measures and commitments of the previous agreements, including and specifically those of the Hebron Note for the Record, but it went into still greater detail regarding each of the measures. Most notably in this connection, the Memorandum provided a detailed list of Palestinian security obligations; it made no such list regarding Israeli obligations. The Memorandum also reiterated the commitment "immediately to resume" final status negotiations, with the addition that these talks were to be "continuous and uninterrupted" with a final accord to be reached by 4 May 1999. Thus the original target date of Oslo was to be honored, and the problem of delays and disruptions, usually connected with terrorist attacks or Israeli complaints, was to be eliminated.

An important innovation of the Wye document was the specification of the percentages of the West Bank to be evacuated instead of the more ambiguous formulation to "specified military locations." Beyond that, the most important innovations were: a strict timeline and introduction of a third party, the United States, for monitoring or some kind of assistance. The timeline broke down all of the obligations into a twelve-week period, the implication being that the steps of each period, though designated as belonging to "week two," or "weeks two-six," etc., would be dependant upon completion of the steps of the previous period. Thus, small portions of the total thirteen percent redeployment were dispersed over the twelve-week timeline, along with steps such as anti-incitement efforts, weapons collection, Charter changes, and police list.. It was clear, even in the negotiations for the Memorandum, that the sequential nature of the timeline would give Israel the possibility of disrupting the process if the Palestinians did not meet the obligations of each step.[21] Netanyahu could and did hold up withdrawals in accord with what he saw as lack of Palestinian "compliance." Unlike the Hebron Note, there was no mention of implementation in parallel.

The United States was written into the process in a number of ways, such as an American promise to "facilitate" the final status negotiations and regular briefings for the Americans regarding the determination of the future rede-ployment. The latter was an implicit expression of the Americans' earlier dis-satisfaction with Netanyahu's avoidance of the redeployment obligations and meant to allay some of the Palestinian concerns that there would still be more foot-dragging about the remaining withdrawal once (if) the Israeli redeploy-ment commitment called for in the Memorandum were met. Beyond these matters, the American role was interjected primarily into the security obliga-tions placed upon the Palestinians. In essence, the Palestinians were to report to the Americans weekly, regarding their actions against terrorism, terrorist infrastructure and suspected terrorists. In addition, these and related security measures were to be reported no less than bi-weekly to a high-level tripartite security cooperation and coordination committee, composed of Americans, Israelis and Palestinians. The Americans would also assist in the collection of weapons[22] and provide technical assistance to the Palestinian police, while they were to be briefed as to the implementation of the measures regarding the police (presumably the reduction of their numbers and weapons, as de-manded by Israel). Further, the United States would participate in a tripartite committee to monitor and prevent incitement. There was nothing to pre-vent this committee from dealing with Israeli incitement, but its creation was clearly a response to Israel's complaints.[23]

The introduction of the United States directly into the process was not necessarily something either Israel or the Palestinians wanted. Israel tradi-tionally was unwilling to have third party supervision or control, and the Pal-estinians, while usually seeking international involvement, believed the U.S. to be biased toward Israel, and further they wanted to avoid an appearance of being under U.S. control. However, Netanyahu presumably did not want to appear to be placing his trust in the Palestinians regarding security issues (the way, according to him and the right-wing, Rabin had done) so the American involvement, in this case, was suitable for Israel, especially since it was limited to supervising Palestinian not Israeli compliance and presented in the form of CIA assistance to a security plan devised by CIA Director George Tenet. Nonetheless, such involvement could have meant that Netanyahu could not get away with unfounded accusations or unreasonable demands. Yet he could also use it as a "guarantee" of Palestinian compliance. For their part, the Palestinians accepted the CIA role as part of Tenet's plan, preferring perhaps to deal directly with Tenet rather than the Israelis.[24] Yet they probably had no choice in the matter, although they managed to prevent direct U.S. involvement in the collection of Palestinian weapons. Thus, a potentially important innovation, the introduction of some instrument for monitoring implementation so starkly missing from the Oslo Accords (with the exception of the virtually powerless TIPH), was conceived and injected mainly to serve Israel's purposes.

The Memorandum also specified that President Clinton himself would participate in a second abrogation of the anti-Israel clauses of the PLO Charter. Netanyahu had demanded a reaffirmation of the vote already taken by the PNC, and the Memorandum called for a meeting to be addressed by Clinton for this purpose. The Likud argument had been that unless the PLO produced a new charter without the offensive clauses, the 1996 PNC resolution to remove these clauses would not constitute fulfillment of the promise made in Arafat's Oslo letter and the Interim Agreement. Yet the Memorandum only reaffirmed Arafat's written assurance to Clinton that the clauses had been abrogated. There was nothing about a new charter. In a highly publicized spectacle, Clinton indeed traveled to Gaza and appeared before the PNC and many dignitaries who then demonstratively reaffirmed the previous resolution by a massive raising of hands.[25]

This was almost the only part of the Wye Memorandum implemented. A month after the Memorandum was signed, Israel belatedly carried out the first piece of the redeployment called for in the timetable, shifting two percent (not the promised twelve percent) of the West Bank from area C to area B and seven percent (not 14.2%) from area B to full Palestinian control. And then Netanyahu stopped the redeployments and suspended the Wye River Memorandum. He had released some prisoners and permitted the opening of the airport in Gaza, but he claimed that the Palestinians had not taken the necessary steps, particularly in the area of security.

The suspension of the Memorandum seemed to confirm the possible interpretation that Netanyahu had been pressured into continuing the peace process and conceding territory, both in the Hebron Agreement and Wye River Memorandum, without either wanting or even intending to meet these obligations. Ideologically, he was hardly one to resist opposition to the agreement from his party and the rest of the right wing. Two months after signing the agreement and one month after suspending it, he was forced to dissolve the Knesset and call new elections.

In September 1999, there was one more attempt to save the Oslo Accords. Ehud Barak, elected Prime Minister in May 1999, signed a new agreement called the **Sharm el-Sheikh Memorandum**[26] updating the timeline and most importantly calling for the drafting of a framework for a final accord within five months (albeit a new, additional agreement) and the conclusion of the final status agreement within a year. However, preferring to conduct negotiations with Syria first, Barak delayed the new timeline's redeployments, finally carried out one more stage of the thirteen percent redeployment promised at Wye River, and then, in January, announced to Arafat that the remaining stage plus the last as yet undetermined redeployment would be skipped since the final status talks, now getting underway, would take care of the matter. This issue, basically the location of the remaining 6.1% to be transferred to the Palestinians under Wye (without mention of the final unspecified redeployment), was bitterly negotiated via the Americans over the next months but the transfer never took place.

▪ Conclusions

The failure to complete the withdrawals was certainly a factor in the failure of the Oslo Accords, but there were several other factors. The DOP and the subsequent agreements were flawed: the interim nature of Oslo opened the way for opponents to provoke and cause disruptions of the process; the agreements provided no clear indication of the endgame, namely the goal of statehood that might have given the Palestinians greater incentive or aided them in implementation; and the agreements neglected to provide a forceful, overall monitoring mechanism to ensure implementation and to prevent the numerous delays and need for even more formal agreements. A number of clauses simply had not been implemented, such as the release of prisoners, provision of safe passage between the Gaza Strip and the West Bank, the building of a seaport and many others. The absence of a direct interdiction on settlement building meant that settlements could and were expanded (virtually doubling the number of settlers), with still more expropriations of land for settlement expansion and for the building of by-pass roads. The Israeli effort to exclude East Jerusalem from Palestinian jurisdiction and its refusal to discuss the city led to the closure of East Jerusalem to non-resident Palestinians, along with periodic closures and road-blocks within the West Bank and Gaza Strip, in part connected with the redeployments and bypass roads, all of which contributed to limitations on Palestinian freedom of movement. Moreover, the Palestinians felt that they were being called upon to protect the Israelis, i.e., to prevent terrorism (which they argued the Israeli army, in full control of the territories, had not been able to do), and that they were losing domestic political support for attempting to do so. Thus, in Palestinian eyes they were actually losing out as a result of Oslo while Israel was the real and only beneficiary.

Israel did indeed benefit from Oslo: Israel's pariah status on the world scene was ended, along with most of the indirect and some direct Arab boycotts; Israel doubled the number of countries with which it had diplomatic relations, it got a peace treaty with Jordan, investment and tourism skyrocketed, including tourism with some Arab countries, all leading to an economic boom for the Israelis

Yet the Palestinians too contributed to the failure of Oslo. There were indeed Palestinian violations, most connected with security matters of concern to Israel such as the size of the police, the number of weapons they held, the apprehension and extradition of suspected terrorists and the like. The most serious Israeli grievance revolved around the actual acts of terrorism, and these in turn strengthened the political opposition leading to a return to power of the right-wing and providing "justification" for the new, ideologically anti-Oslo government to virtually halt the process. The advent of Barak's premiership not only failed to correct the above shortcomings and grievances (indeed Barak expanded settlement building, for example), but also introduced a new concept of the peace process, preferring the Syrian track and jettisoning the remainder of Oslo in favor, belatedly, of accelerated final status negotiations.

CHAPTER THREE

Camp David July 2000

In the months prior to the Camp David summit 11–24 July 2000, there were a number of official and unofficial meetings between Israeli and Palestinian negotiators. However, the failure to reach even minimal agreement, together with the impending end of President Clinton's tenure in office, led to the convening of the summit. Arafat maintained that it was too early for such a meeting—the logic of a summit being to finalize matters more or less agreed upon previously. Nonetheless, Barak pressed both the United States and the Palestinians to hold the meeting primarily because of the soon-to-be-held American elections but, presumably, also because of his promise to reach peace with the Palestinians within one and a half years of his election. The failure of the Camp David talks may have been due to this factor: the fact that one side did not feel that the ground had been sufficiently prepared for such a summit. Many analyses attribute the failure to the personalities involved, particularly the personality of Barak (he did not even meet for direct negotiations with Arafat at Camp David), or to cultural differences and negotiating strategies, or other subjective as well as objective conditions, amongst them the fact that Barak went to the summit in a politically weak position at home.

Although there were official note-takers at some of the meetings, no protocols are available; there are many versions of the talks and of what was or
was not agreed upon there.[1] The differing versions are the result not only of
varied interpretations by the participants, their advisors and outside observers, but also due to the fact that there were a number of small groups and
individuals holding talks and offering proposals, sometimes simultaneously,
during the two weeks. On occasion, agreements were reached but rejected
by the respective leaders; on occasion, there were retreats from positions
already accepted or offered. Therefore, the many versions notwithstanding,
it is almost impossible to determine just which proposals were "official" or
"final" and exactly how they were received. Moreover, each side—even each
participant—had his own political interests, dictating his post-summit version
of what actually *was* put on the table at Camp David.

A significant but unnoted precedent set at the talks was President Clinton's reference, on more than one occasion, to the creation of a Palestinian
state. While not official statements, these comments represented a change in
positions expressed by US presidents in the past. It was this goal that had been
missing from Oslo, but it was clearly understood in the Camp David talks as
the intended final status of the occupied territories, the details and parameters
of which were the topic of the negotiations.

In general, it could be said that the issue on which Camp David failed was
(East) Jerusalem, and particularly the Temple Mount/Haram al-Sharif. There
was not necessarily agreement on all the other issues—refugees, borders,
security—but the two sides appeared to come quite close to agreement on
these matters (with positions we shall discuss below), while the Jerusalem issue
was the one that prevented the drafting of a final agreement of any kind.

Barak's "Offer": On 18 July, the eighth day of deliberations and after many
proposals and disputes as well as informal agreements below the level of the
leadership, Barak gave Clinton his "bottom lines" regarding most of the issues,
to be presented to Arafat by the American president ostensibly as positions
he, Clinton, would "try" to achieve from Barak.[2] In fact, Barak subsequently
modified this offer and even retreated from some aspects, but it is significant
as the "best" Israeli offer presented.

Regarding Jerusalem, Barak accepted an arrangement proposed by the Americans, namely that of Palestinian "custodianship" of the Temple Mount; Palestinian sovereignty in the Muslim and Christian quarters of the Old City and in seven of the eight or nine outer neighborhoods of East Jerusalem plus functional autonomy (zoning, planning, security, law enforcement) in the inner ring of East Jerusalem.[3] Regarding borders, Israel would annex nine percent of the West Bank in exchange for the equivalent of one percent to be given the Palestinians south of Gaza—the idea of swapping territory. Security matters were not detailed in this offer, but in general there was acceptance of an international presence for the international borders while Israel would, nonetheless, maintain control of part of the Jordan (Rift) Valley amounting to an additional ten percent of the West Bank for no more than twelve years. The refugee issue would be resolved in a manner satisfactory to both sides.

According to this offer, the Palestinian state would consist of the Gaza Strip, ninety-one percent of the West Bank and an area south of the Gaza Strip equivalent to one percent of the West Bank. In other words, the "swaps" were to be nine to one in Israel's favor, and the Palestinian state would be roughly eight percent less than the area envisaged in their "mini-state" compromise (the 1988 decision to accept twenty-two percent of Mandated Palestine for their state). It was on the basis of this decision that the Palestinian position, presented from Oslo onward, was that the occupied territories (West Bank and Gaza) were not negotiable; the only border was to be the 4 June 1967 line or the equivalent by means of land swaps. For this reason, Barak's territorial offer was rejected. Swaps, which were to accommodate Israeli retention of the majority of Jewish settlers (the nine percent was to consist of settlement blocs which could contain some eighty percent of the settlers), had to be equal, according to the Palestinians.

On the issue of security, the idea of an international presence (instead of an Israeli presence) was a compromise on Barak's part, as was the agreement to give up all of the Jordan Valley after a number of years. The Labor Party had consistently delineated this area, which constitutes part of the border with Jordan, as one that Israel must retain in any agreement. Hence the demand to hold on to at least part of this area, even if only for a limited time (and indeed the first Israeli offer regarding this area called for Israeli control

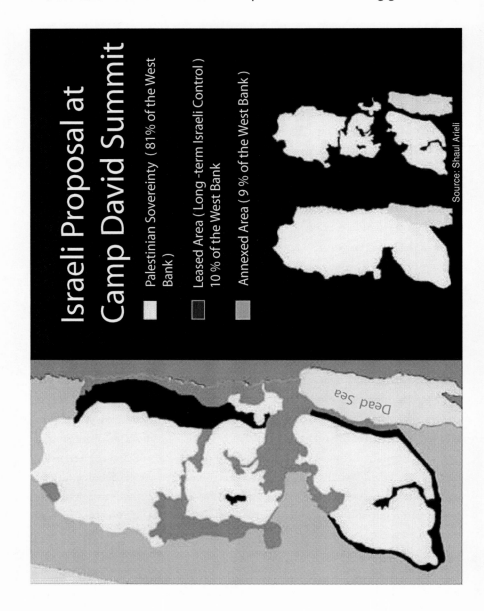

for twenty to thirty years). Refusal to give it up altogether, however, would have meant continued Israeli control over the borders of the Palestinian state on the West Bank.

While not specified in Barak's proposal, one of the security matters proposed by the Israelis was the retention of five early warning posts in the West Bank (subsequently reduced to three)—a demand accepted in principle by the Palestinians at least at one point in the negotiations. However, the Palestinians did not like the idea of these posts being connected by roads that would come under Israeli control in case of emergencies. From the Palestinian point of view, this would violate Palestinian sovereignty, potentially cutting the West Bank into separate areas on each side of these main roads leading from Israel to the eastern border.

Barak's offer said virtually nothing regarding the refugee issue (just "satisfactory solution") presumably for a number of reasons. The refugee issue in many ways had long been the one issue that might strike at the very existence of the State of Israel, and for this reason it had remained unresolved from the creation of the refugee problem in 1947–48 to the present. If Israel were to permit the return of the refugees—whether the numbers were close to the original 600,000–700,000 (in 1949) or the 3–4 million claimed today—this would create a situation whereby Jews would be a minority in Israel sooner or later. Few if any Jewish Israelis would agree to such a situation. Thus the Israeli position, historically and at Camp David, was that the UN Resolution 194, which allowed for the refugees' return should not be interpreted as according a "right." Actually Israel preferred to avoid any reference to Resolution 194 since it was indeed interpreted by the Palestinians and others as the basis for the "right of return" of the refugees. Moreover, the resolution specified the refugees' return "to their homes," not, as Israel might have preferred, a more general "return" to the Palestinian homeland or Palestine which could be interpreted as the future Palestinian state that would come in the West Bank and Gaza. Resolution 194 also stipulated that compensation should be forthcoming from the "governments and authorities responsible." Israel consistently denied any responsibility, although at Camp David it was willing to agree to participate in international funding of compensation, as well as permit a small number of refugees to enter Israel under family reunification (a system that had been in effect for some time now, in any case).

The Palestinian position at Camp David was simply that Resolution 194 was the only basis for a solution to the refugee problem, and Israel must assume its responsibility particularly with regard to compensation. Although this position was stated, the impression of both the Americans and the Israelis, from informal talks before and at Camp David, was that Arafat was not going to make an issue of this problem.[4] And the Palestinians did offer to negotiate the implementation of Resolution 194 in a manner that would meet Israel's demographic and security interests (for example, limiting numbers of returnees). Presumably, for these reasons as well, Barak did not go beyond the general formulation ("satisfactory solution"). At the end of the talks, when it appeared that no agreement was forthcoming, the Palestinians asserted a more uncompromising position, namely, the demand that every refugee be given the right to return home.

Jerusalem had become a sensitive issue for Israel (as well as the Palestinians). Originally, according to the 1947 UN Partition Plan, Jerusalem was to have become an international city because of its importance to the three major religions. As a result of the battles in the 1948 war, Jordan extended its control over the eastern part of the cityincluding the Old City, and Israel over the western part. Each state then annexed its part, and Israel declared (west) Jerusalem its capital, though this status was never recognized by the international community (with the exception, for a number of years, of El Salvador and Costa Rica). In the 1967 war, Israel captured East Jerusalem from the Jordanians, dismantled the wall that had separated the two parts of the city and annexed the eastern part, while expanding the borders of the entire city;[5] in 1980 Israel gave this legal status as "united Jerusalem, the capital of Israel."

Jewish settlement of the eastern part, particularly the outlying areas, parts of the Old City and especially the old Jewish Quarter, was undertaken with parallel efforts to limit the Palestinian presence in the city. The Oslo Accords, as already noted, left the Jerusalem issue for the final status talks but, upon Israel's insistence, explicitly excluded Jerusalem from the jurisdiction of the Palestinian Authority and from other measures. Nonetheless, during the Oslo period right-wing political propaganda continuously accused the Labor Party

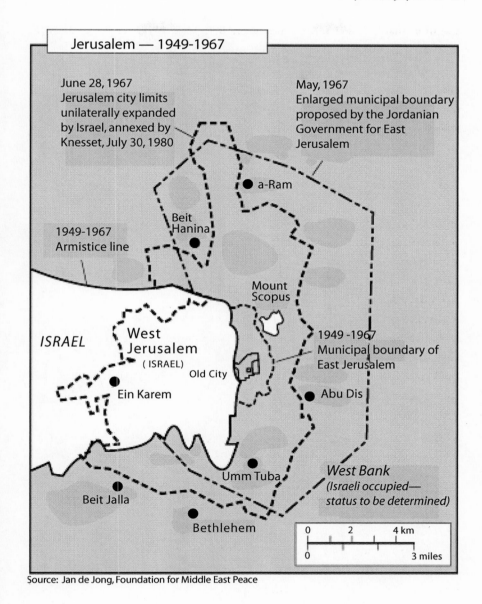

Jerusalem — 1949-1967

June 28, 1967
Jerusalem city limits
unilaterally expanded
by Israel, annexed by
Knesset, July 30, 1980

May, 1967
Enlarged municipal boundary
proposed by the Jordanian
Government for East
Jerusalem

● a-Ram

1949-1967
Armistice line

Beit
Hanina ●

Mount
Scopus

ISRAEL

West
Jerusalem
(ISRAEL)

Old City

1949 -1967
Municipal boundary of
East Jerusalem

● Ein Karem

● Abu Dis

● Umm Tuba

West Bank
(Israeli occupied—
status to be determined)

● Beit Jalla

● Bethlehem

0   2   4 km

0   3 miles

Source: Jan de Jong, Foundation for Middle East Peace

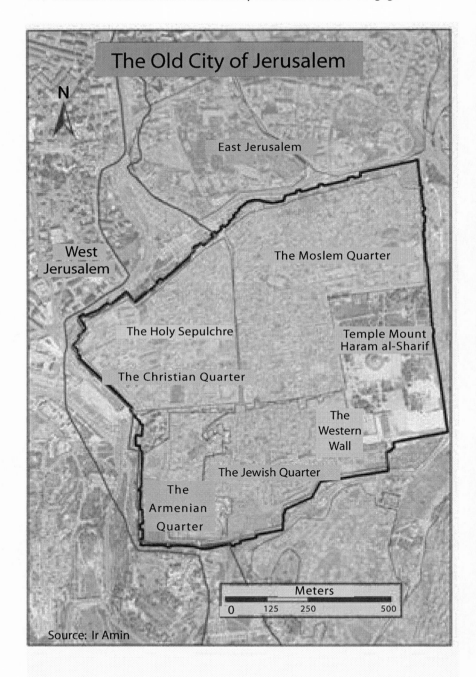

The Old City of Jerusalem

N

East Jerusalem

West Jerusalem

The Moslem Quarter

The Holy Sepulchre

Temple Mount
Haram al-Sharif

The Christian Quarter

The Western Wall

The Jewish Quarter

The Armenian Quarter

Meters

0   125   250   500

Source: Ir Amin

or its leaders of planning to divide Jerusalem. This accusation rendered the Jerusalem issue even more sensitive for Labor negotiators. The specific area of the Temple Mount/Haram al-Sharif was not actually a major issue going into the Camp David talks, but it was a sensitive one. The Haram al-Sharif held a place of some importance in Islam, which meant that it was an issue of interest to a far broader public of Muslims than just the Palestinians. At the same time, the Temple Mount (the site of the biblical temple of the Israelites), upon which the mosques of the Haram al-Sharif were situated, had assumed the symbolic role for Israelis of the Jewish link to Jerusalem and even to the Land of Israel.

Barak's formulation for Jerusalem, noted above, was virtually word for word a proposal raised by the Americans. It accorded far more than the Israeli team had been advocating until then. Actually Barak had sought to avoid any discussion of Jerusalem, but the Israeli team had come around gradually to an idea of expanding the borders of Jerusalem (already expanded by Israel after the 1967 war) to include the East Jerusalem suburb of Abu Dis and then have Abu Dis proclaimed the capital of the Palestinian state with administrative jurisdiction over East Jerusalem. They had also come around to the idea of Palestinian sovereignty over certain areas in the outlying Arab areas of East Jerusalem. The American proposal accepted by Barak went a bit further as noted above. Nonetheless, it fell far short of the Palestinians' demand for all of East Jerusalem (with the possible exception of the Jewish Quarter of the Old City and the Western Wall) to come under Palestinian sovereignty and form the capital of the Palestinian state. Moreover, the idea of Palestinian custodianship of the Temple Mount/Haram al-Sharif was no more than the already existing situation, with continued Israeli sovereignty deemed totally unacceptable by Arafat—and possibly by the Muslim world as well.

Thus, Arafat rejected Barak's offer (the whole offer) as presented to him by President Clinton. He raised some questions on various issues, but the main sticking point was the Jerusalem issue, specifically the matter of the Haram al-Sharif. While there was a serious crisis in the talks over Arafat's rejection, the Palestinian team offered some alternative ideas regarding Jerusalem, and negotiations finally continued. But the offer placed on the table by Barak underwent significant changes. Regarding the borders, Israeli territorial demands went up as high as 13.3% and finally settled, by the end of the talks, at 10–12% depending on how specific areas were calculated (for example, with or without the areas for safe passage between Gaza and the West Bank). Barak rejected the counter map presented by the Palestinians by which the Palestinians would receive all of the West Bank, with some settlements connected by roads to Israel (accommodating only thirty percent rather than eighty percent of the settlers). No agreement was reached on the borders. There are contradictory accounts as to whether the Palestinians agreed to Israeli use of airspace for security purposes without interfering with commercial air traffic. Israel wanted such an arrangement; the Palestinians reportedly rejected it, though there was some agreement regarding Israeli flights and something close to demilitarization of the Palestinian state as well. Similarly, although there was no agreement regarding water rights, there was the sense that agreement could be reached on this matter.

While there was little if any agreement on most of the issues, the final effort concentrated on Jerusalem in the belief that if this issue could be resolved, negotiations would move positively on all the other issues. There was a slight improvement in Barak's Jerusalem offer (sovereignty in some areas of the inner circle of Jerusalem and a Presidential Compound for the Palestinians in the Old City), but the Israelis also added the demand that Jews have the right to pray on the Temple Mount/Haram al-Sharif and continued to insist on maintaining Israeli sovereignty over that area. Clinton suggested several innovative ideas for the problem, such as dividing sovereignty over the Temple Mount/Haram al-Sharif, but neither side was satisfied. With the failure of this final effort to reach agreement on this small but critical area of Jerusalem, the talks ended, with tragic repercussions in the following months.

It is hard to point to any real agreement on the issues of final status at Camp David, despite the fact that the negotiators themselves believed that progress had been made on most issues. Barak did indeed make an offer, however reluctantly, that went well beyond anything any Israeli prime minister had been willing to concede in the past, particularly with regard to Jerusalem. Yet it clearly fell short of what Arafat was willing to accept. And the Palestinian counter proposals fell far short of what Barak was willing to accept. It has been said that the Palestinians viewed the situation as asymmetric: they were the victims, Israel was holding the Palestinians' lands, the Palestinians were merely demanding their rights (having already conceded seventy-eight percent of their lands)—and therefore Israel had to make the moves. The Israelis, and perhaps the Americans, saw the negotiations as if among equals: one side makes a concession, the other side responds with a concession, the result being not a matter of rights but of compromise, with both sides moving.[6] The Americans found both leaders, at times, to be unjustifiably stubborn and unbending, but ultimately Clinton placed the burden of blame for the failure solely on the shoulders of Arafat. In part this was done to assist Barak politically at home, so that he might be able to maintain his government and resume negotiations in the future. However, this had the opposite effect, for by blaming Arafat—as both Clinton and Barak did—they created a situation in which the public response was not in support of further negotiations but rather the conclusion that it was impossible to make peace with Arafat. This widespread attitude was compounded by the failure to fully reveal just what was discussed at Camp David, which made Palestinian refusal nearly incomprehensible. Indeed most Israelis, according to the polls in the weeks after Camp David, believed that Barak had been too generous.[7] Moreover, comments made by various Israelis that the talks had collapsed over a Palestinian demand for the right of return for all the refugees—a demand that struck at the very existence of the state of Israel—revived the old fears and beliefs in Israel that the Palestinians' ultimate goal was not peace but the dismantling of the State of Israel. The result: widespread conviction among the Israeli public that there was no partner for peace. The outbreak of the al-Aksa Intifada two months later provided "proof" for this conviction.

The outbreak of the Intifada was in part due to Palestinian reactions to Camp David which were similar to those of the Israelis. For much the same reason, namely the fact that full information on just what went on at Camp David had not been forthcoming, the Palestinian public had its own version of Barak's offer.[8] In their eyes, Barak had offered only a truncated Palestinian state that would be split into three (four with Gaza) "cantons" by Israeli controlled roads crossing from Israel in the west to the eastern border, and Israel continuing to control the eastern border for a long period of time. In this version, Israel would also have maintained control of the airspace above and the water resources below the West Bank, and the land swaps, grossly unequal to begin with (nine to one) would have given the Palestinians only a poor patch of desert land south of the Gaza Strip while Israel took a large junk of the West Bank, maintaining many settlements. In addition Israel would keep East Jerusalem, permitting only isolated "ghettos" for the Palestinians.

A widespread conclusion among the Palestinian public was that Barak had not come to Camp David to negotiate; not only did he present a "take it or leave it" offer, but that he knew the offer could not be accepted. Clinton was viewed as entirely loyal to the Israelis, and for many, Camp David appeared to have been almost a conspiracy to discredit the Palestinians and provide an excuse for Israel to maintain its occupation.[9] Combined with the deep disappointment over the failure of the Oslo Accords to improve Palestinian lives (much less end the occupation) and the facts Israel was creating on the ground, namely the continued settlement building and expropriation of land, the failure at Camp David was apparently the final measure in Palestinian frustration.

It took only a minor spark, the ill-advised visit to the Temple Mount (al-Aksa mosque area) by Sharon (head of the Opposition in the Israeli Knesset at that time), to set off the violence of the al-Aksa Intifada. Some claim that Arafat favored an Intifada as a lever to get a better deal from Barak. This may or may not have been the case, just as it is still not clear to many as to whether Arafat ordered the Intifada or merely acquiesced to it once it broke out. However, the outbreak of the Intifada was incomprehensible to most Israelis, who for the most part, and based on very scanty knowledge of what actually did happen at Camp David, believed that Barak had made a very generous offer and Arafat had refused it. Even many in the Israeli peace camp believed that Barak's concessions, so far as they were known, were at least a basis for continued negotiations rather than a reason for reverting to violence. The violence, on both sides, became the worst either Israelis or Palestinians had experienced in their long conflict, bringing Sharon to power in Israel and with this a tragic retreat from any negotiations or peace process.

CHAPTER FOUR

The Clinton Parameters—December 2000

Despite the failure of Camp David and the impending termination of his time in office, Clinton did not abandon his efforts to bring about an agreement. There were a number of talks, between both Israelis and Palestinians and each of them with American mediators, including even a summit in October for the purpose of ending the violence. The result of all this came on 23 December 2000 when Clinton provided Barak and Arafat with what he saw as a basis for agreement on key issues. This became known as the Clinton Bridging Proposals or the Clinton Parameters. Clinton made it clear to both sides that he did not want them to negotiate over his points but rather accept them as a basis to be refined in subsequent talks. The idea was to provide a means of bridging between the positions of the two sides, building on things that had been agreed or nearly agreed upon previously and meeting the basic needs of each side, at least as these had become clearer in the previous talks.

Speaking clearly of the need for a two-state solution, Clinton suggested, with regard to borders, that Israel withdraw from ninety-four to ninety-six percent of the West Bank with a land swap equal to one to three percent of the area as compensation to the Palestinians. The actual map to be drawn up by the two would follow the criteria of territorial contiguity for the Palestinians, accommodation of eighty percent of the settlers in blocs annexed by Israel, but minimal annexation and minimum number of Palestinians affected by Israeli annexation. This would almost be squaring the circle—that is, accommodating eighty percent of the setters in no more than six percent of the land, which would accord the Palestinians the equivalent of a minimum of ninety-five percent and possibly even ninety-nine percent of the territory. Israel had already indicated to the Americans that ninety-five percent was more than it wanted to give up and its absolute bottom line; Clinton subsequently said his parameters would give the Palestinians ninety-seven percent including the swaps.

The key to the security arrangements would be an "international presence," agreed to in principle earlier by both sides. Such a unit would gradually replace Israeli forces over a three-year period, with a limited Israeli presence remaining in the Jordan Valley for no more than an additional three years (instead of the minimum twelve years Israel had urged at Camp David), under the authority of the international force. The international force would be removed only upon the agreement of both sides. While this was something of a move in the Palestinian direction, Clinton added an Israeli right to re-enter, presumably using the roads to the Jordan Valley, in case of emergency. Clinton said that the term "emergency" would need to be clearly defined (for example, imminent threat to Israel's national security), but such Israeli access might still be perceived by the Palestinians as a threat to their sovereignty.

Israel would maintain only three early warning posts, with Palestinian liaison personnel present. These posts would be reviewed after ten years and removed only with the agreement of both sides. The Palestinians would maintain total sovereignty over their airspace but they would be required to work out some arrangement for Israeli training and operational needs. Finally, the Palestinian state would be more or less "demilitarized" but the term would be "non-militarized" to indicate that the Palestinians would have a strong security force in addition to the international force that would be there for border security and deterrence purposes. On the whole, these points met all of Israel's basic security needs but in a way that provided somewhat less than what Israel wanted while responding at least in part to Palestinian sensitivities

Map Reflecting Clinton Ideas

Proposed Palestinian State

Israeli Settlement Blocs Annexed to Israel

Haifa

Sea of Galilee

Mediterannean Sea

Jenin

Tulkarm

Nablus

Qalqilya

Jordan River

Tel Aviv

WEST BANK

Ramallah

Jericho

Jerusalem

Ma'aleh Adumim

ISRAEL

Bethlehem

Gaza

Hebron

Gaza Strip

Dead Sea

JORDAN

EGYPT

No formal map was presented to the Israelis and Palestinians in December 2000 by President Clinton, but this map illustrates the Clinton ideas, without the land to be swapped from from Israel to the Palestinian state.

Source: Mideastnet (www.mideastnet.com)

about sovereignty. The major concession Israel would be making in the security area, aside from the time period and number of outposts involved, would be the idea of an international force. Israel had agreed to an international "presence" (already a concession if it were to replace an Israeli presence), but in the past, at least, Israel had been most shy of an actual "force." The Palestinians had always sought an international presence, though for the border they would have preferred solely Palestinian control. However, the fact that the force would replace Israel and supervise implementation (not stated explicitly in the parameters but understood) promised to provide the much needed verification that had been missing from Oslo (and possibly keep Israel from re-entering).

The most difficult points were, of course, the refugees and Jerusalem. There was no room for compromise with Israel on the right of return. Clinton made that quite clear and came up with two proposals, both based on the idea of the refugee issue being resolved basically within the Palestinian state. The formulation could be either recognition by both sides of the Palestinian refugees' "right to return to historic Palestine" or "the right of the Palestinian refugees to their homeland." In either case, no question would be left as to the locale intended. Moreover, according to Clinton, Israel had the right to determine its immigration policy and to preserve its Jewish character. Assuming that Israel might let some refugees in, he proposed the five options often discussed in the past: "return" to the Palestinian state; "return" to areas being transferred to the Palestinians in the land swap; integration into the countries they presently were in; resettlement in a third country; admission to Israel. The last three would depend upon the immigration policies of the countries involved, including Israel. Priority would be given to the refugees in Lebanon whose plight was perhaps the worst and who were mainly from families still in the Galilee area of Israel. Taken together, all these steps were to be viewed as implementing Resolution 194.

While this proposal was not new, and was most likely privately understood by the Palestinians to be the best they could ever get, it would still be a difficult one for them to accept. The refugee issue was no less sensitive for the Palestinians than it was for Israelis. Arafat had negotiated all the Oslo agreements without regard for the refugees, and the Palestinian Authority represented only those Palestinians in the occupied territories; the PLO, on whose behalf Arafat also spoke, theoretically represented all Palestinians—and many abroad had not been happy with the neglect of the refugee problem. The trade-off for Arafat would appear to have been Clinton's proposals regarding Jerusalem. His ideas for Jerusalem ignored all the complicated geographic arrangements proffered by the Israelis at Camp David, and the ideas clearly moved in the direction of the Palestinians' demands. Quite simply, Clinton suggested: the Arab neighborhoods would be under Palestinian sovereignty; Jewish neighborhoods under Israeli sovereignty. With regard to the delicate issue of the Temple Mount/Haram al-Sharif, two solutions were offered: either Palestinian sovereignty over the Haram al-Sharif and Israeli sovereignty over the Western Wall (and the space around it) accompanied by a commitment not to excavate below the Haram or behind the Wall; or the same arrangement of sovereignty plus "shared functional sovereignty" regarding excavations—meaning mutual consent would be necessary for any excavations. The Palestinians would get their capital in Jerusalem, genuinely, while Israel, as Clinton put it, would finally get recognition of quite a large part of Jerusalem as its capital.

Together all these points would culminate in an agreement that the conflict between Israel and the Palestinians was over, and the relevant UN resolutions implemented. According to Clinton, inasmuch as the Israeli withdrawal was to be spread over three years, presumably at the end of this time the Palestinian state would be established—although this was not stated explicitly.

It was merely left for Barak and Arafat to notify Clinton (within four days) as to their acceptance or rejection of these parameters. Barak accepted the parameters by the date set by Clinton, but Arafat did not. Cynics might say Barak accepted them because he knew Arafat would not. Certainly the parameters did not meet all of Barak's demands, either on territory or security or, especially, Jerusalem. But already facing a tough election battle at home, in the face of increasing violence, he saw this as the last opportunity to have Clinton's backing. Arafat did not reject the parameters outright, but rather he expressed numerous reservations that negated most of the proposals, and he withheld any final answer, negative or positive. Arafat's reservations included everything from the Israeli presence in the Jordan Valley to the arrangements in Jerusalem, the discussion of the implementation of the right of return, and the matter of the airspace.[1] Even explanations that the parameters would mean a Palestinian state in as much as ninety-seven percent of the territories did not prompt a clear or positive response from him. Clinton and others have indicated that many of the Palestinian negotiators wanted to accept the parameters. And indeed, the parameters themselves did not die.[2] They were to return indirectly in the Taba talks, conducted without the Americans, and they could easily be discerned in the track-two Geneva Initiative produced in 2003.

CHAPTER FIVE

Taba—January 2001

The 18–27 January 2001 talks at Taba were a last-ditch attempt to reach an agreement of some kind just weeks before Barak was to face Sharon in the Israeli elections. Arafat was particularly interested in holding the talks, believing according to some, that Barak would be re-elected (despite all the polls to the contrary) and would, therefore, stand behind an agreement if reached. It has also been claimed that he thought the new Bush administration would be favorable (in view of the policies pursued by Bush Sr.), particularly if inheriting a peace plan already more or less agreed upon.[1] For his part, Barak did not believe an agreement could be reached, particularly since Arafat still refrained from accepting the Clinton parameters. His colleagues, however, prevailed upon him to make one last attempt, and he may have agreed to do so in the belief that success, if achieved, might save the election for him. For this reason Barak sent what has been called the "dream team," namely the leading supporters of peace in his cabinet: Yossi Beilin, Shlomo Ben-Ami, Yossi Sarid, and former Israeli army (IDF) chief of staff Amnon Lipkin-Shahak. As in the case of Camp David, so too with regard to Taba, no single official version of what was or was not achieved there exists. Participant accounts vary, and the only more or less comprehensive account, that of EU observer Miguel Moratinos, represents a composite of his own firsthand observations of the first days of talks and subsequent contributions by some of the participants.[2] There is perhaps more controversy over what was agreed upon at Taba than at Camp David, not only because of the absence of any protocols or written papers (with the exception of drafts on the refugee issue), but mainly because the only written official or semi-official accounts, namely the final press statement delivered by Abu Ala and the Moratinos summary have been challenged by a number of participants in various ways.[3]

The context of the talks was perhaps one of the most unpropitious that one could have sought: there were almost daily Palestinian terror attacks against Israelis within Israel and the occupied territories;[4] there was the mounting use of the Israeli army and air force against Palestinians in the territories, with an ever increasing death toll; the Israeli leader, Barak, was weeks from an election that he was more or less certain to lose; the Palestinian leader, Arafat, was under totally conflicting pressures at home and abroad; public opinion in each community was convinced that the other side was uncompromising and unwilling to make peace; the only significant outside mediator, America, was between presidents; and a long line of failed negotiations had preceded the talks even up to the last days. As one observer put it, only the Israeli Peace Now movement continued to advocate publicly for peace, sending a boatload of supporters to the waters outside the Taba Hilton Hotel with banners of encouragement for the negotiators.[5]

With regard to borders, the principle of the 4 June 1967 lines as the guide was accepted. For the first time, an Israeli government was willing to concede this formula in principle (although the negotiations at Camp David and even the Oslo Accords implied this basis). However, the Israelis still attempted to accommodate eighty percent of the settlers in settlement blocs on land to be taken from the West Bank, including land for future expansion of the settlements, and it still offered only unequal swaps in return. The Palestinians initially objected to the idea of settlement blocs, but ultimately acquiesced.[6] They held firm to their demand, again, for land swaps equal in size and quality, with contiguity. However, the new development was the introduction of maps and Palestinian agreement, after numerous proposals, to permit Israel to annex 3.1% of the West Bank (even a suggestion at one point of 4.5% that included the Jewish areas of East Jerusalem). What remains unclear is whether land swaps were to be in addition, as would have been the case with the Clinton parameters, or rather compensation for this 3.1%--meaning that the Palestinians would have what they wanted, the equivalent of 100% of the West Bank (the Gaza Strip was understood all along as 100% Palestinian).

Israeli maps and demands called for six percent of the West Bank, not including Jerusalem neighborhoods or the Latrun salient, which Israel demanded and would bring the total to eight percent. Israel also sought a further two percent to be leased to Israel (apparently for 99 years)—which the Palestinians rejected—but three percent to be returned to the Palestinians in swaps (apparently still the earlier offer of an area south of the Gaza Strip). This did not constitute agreement since there remained a difference of a little less than three percent (excluding the lease demand), but the two sides appeared to be approaching the ninety-seven percent suggested by Clinton, with additional land swaps. This would be more territory than Israel wanted to give up (and more than the maximum Barak had explicitly set for his negotiators), accommodating perhaps only seventy percent of the settlers, and there remained differences over Jewish neighborhoods around and inside East Jerusalem, as well as the lack of clarity regarding the swaps.[7] Nonetheless, the differences appeared to be narrowing, and therefore there was optimism among negotiators on both sides.

Regarding security issues, the Clinton parameters were apparently accepted on the number of Israeli early warning posts (three instead of the five sought by Israel), the non-militarization (or limited militarization) of the Palestinian state, and the international presence (actually referred to as "forces" in the Clinton parameters). Other issues, such as access to Israeli positions (the use of the roads), length of time of Israeli control of the Jordan Valley or of the overall withdrawal, and the airspace question were not sufficiently discussed to reach agreement, each side holding to their earlier, opposing positions.

The Jerusalem issue was discussed in a most detailed way, with far more complex proposals than those raised at Camp David or in the Clinton parameters. However, no agreement was reached. The Israelis apparently ac-

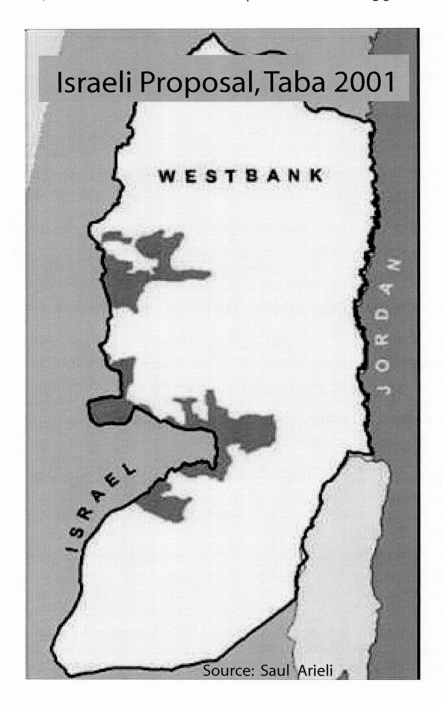

Israeli Proposal, Taba 2001

WESTBANK

JORDAN

ISRAEL

Source: Saul Arieli

cepted Clinton's principle of Arab neighborhoods to the Palestinians, Jewish neighborhoods to Israel, although as noted above the Palestinians counted some of the Jewish neighborhoods of East Jerusalem as part of the territorial agreement, namely the 1.5% that had been added to the 3.1% the Palestinians were willing to leave to Israel.[8] And disputes remained over various neighborhoods and suburbs. However, the major problems, as at Camp David, revolved around the holy sites, particularly the Temple Mount/Haram al-Sharif. Control and management of each side's holy sites could be resolved (with some dispute over the exact areas involved), but the sovereignty issue remained. Proposals for temporary "international sovereignty" over the holy sites, including the Temple Mount/Haram al-Sharif were raised informally, but no agreement was reached, and it is difficult to determine if either side would in fact have agreed to such an arrangement.

The only issue upon which there apparently was significant agreement and for which there were actually written working papers submitted was that of the refugees. Yossi Beilin, who, together with Nebil Sha'ath, conducted the working group on this topic at Taba has provided an account of the understandings reached.[9] As in the Clinton parameters, the refugees in Lebanon were the main concern.[10] The solution would be the five options offered in the Clinton parameters: refugees to the Palestinian state and to the areas transferred to the Palestinians in the swaps, absorption in the countries in which they already resided, immigration to a third country such as Canada, the U.S. or European countries, and a limited number to Israel. In addition, Israel would continue its policy of family reunification. In his own accounts, Beilin does not mention a more detailed proposal which Moritanos claims was raised by the Israelis informally: Israel would absorb 25,000 refugees over a three-year period, then another 15,000 in an additional two years, so that the total number of refugees Israel would accept, beyond the usual family reunification process, would be 40,000. However, there was no actual agreement on these or any other specifics such as a timetable or numbers.

Compensation through an international fund, in which Israel would participate, would be worked out and administered by an international organization. This international organization would also deal with rehabilitation of the refugees, gradually replacing UNWRA. Israel proposed that the issue of compensation for properties lost by Jews who left Arab countries also be included in the final agreement. The Palestinians rejected this suggestion on the grounds that this was not a matter for a bilateral Palestinian-Israeli agreement, though it apparently was left for further discussion (at least in the eyes of the Israelis) within the framework of general international compensations.

It was decided that the agreement on refugees would have to include the narratives of each side regarding the differing interpretations of UN Resolution 194 and the responsibility issue, but the suffering of the refugees would be acknowledged and most importantly, Resolution 194 would be viewed as implemented by the measures outlined in the Clinton parameters (which were basically those adopted by the Beilin-Sha'ath working group at Taba). In other words, this solution in its final form would constitute an end to Palestinian claims.

Unfortunately, in the final statement given to the press at the close of the Taba meeting, Abu Ala chose to ignore the progress made on the refugee issue. Providing a generally positive and optimistic account of the meetings, Abu Ala nonetheless decided to mention only the standard Palestinian demand for the right of return and Israel's standard refusal. Although Beilin and Sha'ath objected, Abu Ala apparently believed that revelation of concessions on this point, without full agreement on the whole settlement, would only harm the negotiators' public standing and possibly future negotiations. However, this negative version of the one issue that Israelis viewed as critical to the very existence of the state, and an indication of the Palestinians' true objectives, went a long way to dissipating any positive effect the Taba talks might have had. Still worse, the idea that even the "dream team," Israel's most dovish leaders, could not budge the Palestinians on this critical issue strengthened the already deepening apprehensions of the Israelis and the belief that there was no Palestinian partner for peace.

It is true that the Taba talks did not produce a final agreement, or even the framework agreement sought by Barak at Camp David. Even that which was achieved was not revealed publicly or even acknowledged by both sides. Moreover, there was no certainty that the progress made would, ultimately, have been acceptable to Barak and Arafat. Their respective negotiators had often been closer to agreement in the past than the leaders, particularly regarding the Clinton parameters, and upon occasion they had been more flexible than either Barak or Arafat apparently wanted. This was to have been tested at a summit scheduled for the end of the month, but such a summit never took place. Nevertheless, the Taba talks went a long way toward establishing the Clinton parameters as the basis for an agreement, bringing the Palestinian positions somewhat closer to those of Israel. Indeed participants such as Nabil Sha'ath, Shlomo Ben Ami and Yossi Beilin claimed that the two sides had never been closer to agreement. In its more detailed and informal discussion of the problems, as well as its constructive atmosphere, Taba seemed to contain the potential for an eventual trade-off between Israeli demands regarding Jerusalem on the one hand and Palestinian demands regarding the refugees, on the other hand—a trade-off envisaged by Clinton and very likely the one that would ultimately enable a final Israeli-Palestinian peace agreement. Given the context of the talks, namely both the escalating violence and especially the Israeli elections due in a matter of days which were expected to oust Barak from power, little more could have been expected from Taba.

CHAPTER SIX

Mitchell-Tenet-Zinni Recommendations— April 2001–March 2002

The election of Sharon, the continuation of the Intifada and subsequent Israeli military moves into virtually all of the areas of the Palestine Authority effectively ended any further attempt at official negotiations for a final status agreement. Instead, a number of plans were presented to bring about an end to the violence and a return to the negotiating table. The first of these was contained in the 30 April 2001 *Report of the Sharm el-Sheikh Fact-Finding Committee*, headed by former US Senator George Mitchell (known particularly for his successful peace efforts in Northern Ireland).[1] The Committee, consisting of former Turkish Premier Suleyman Demirel, Norwegian Foreign Minister Thorbjoern Jagland, former US Senator Warren Rudman, and the European Union's Javier Solana, proposed a set of tasks for both Israel and the Palestinians designed to end the violence, build mutual confidence and bring the two sides back to negotiations.

The major recommendations of the Report were divided into three sections: End the Violence, Rebuild Confidence, Resume Negotiations. The first section called for an immediate and unconditional ceasefire to be accompanied by a resumption of Israeli-Palestinian security cooperation. In the

Report, but not in the specific recommendations, each side was expected to assert a 100% effort to prevent violence, defined as "an all-out effort" on the part of the Palestinians to enforce a complete ceasefire and a 100% effort on the Israeli side to ensure that encounters with Palestinians do not lead to renewed hostilities. The Report, but not its recommendations, suggested that the resumption of security cooperation might be facilitated by a third party, with mutual consent of Israel and the Palestinians. The Committee may have had in mind the kind of role accorded the U.S. in the Wye Memorandum, but the Report spoke only vaguely about an outside party to create an "appropriate framework," sustain goodwill on each side, and remove friction where possible, ensuring that its work be perceived as contributing to the welfare and safety of both sides. This was distinct from another idea, that of an international force, that also appeared in the Report, but not the recommendations. Regarding an international force, there was a reference to the temporary observer unit in Hebron (TIPH) and its task of observing and reporting on "explosive situations." Clearly, the Committee was wary of Israel's opposition to outside involvement, particularly in view of the fact that many observers in Israel argued that the Palestinians' goal in the Intifada was to bring about international intervention in order to end the occupation. Indeed the discussion part of the Report referred both to the Palestinians interest in an "international protection force" to protect them, and Israel's opposition to a force of this nature. Presumably for this reason there was no mention of an outside party of any kind in the recommendations.

The ceasefire was to be followed by a cooling-off period consisting of a number of measures designed to rebuild confidence. The recommendations clearly called upon the Palestinians to make a 100% effort to prevent terrorism and punish perpetrators. And both sides were implored to curb incitement in all forms. Together with these measures aimed at rebuilding confidence, the Report recommended that Israel "freeze all settlement activity, including the natural growth of existing settlements." The recommendations elaborated on this point, leaving no doubt that the settlements constituted a major obstacle both to maintaining calm and achieving peace. In this context, the recommendations added a reference to the nature of a final agreement: the suggestion that Israel clarifies to the Palestinians that the future peace agreement would not threaten Palestinian territorial contiguity. This was a mild reference to the Palestinian concern over the settlement blocs and use of roads which would cut the West Bank into cantons—an issue which had been raised in the Camp David talks. Territorial contiguity had now become a standard demand for the Palestinians.

The recommendations carried further proposals that reflected Palestinian concerns, such as a number of demands upon the Israeli army regarding the use of weapons, the treatment of unarmed demonstrators, and the need to apply the IDF's ethical code of conduct. Along with these came recommendations that Israel lift the closures and permit Palestinian laborers back into Israel, transfer tax revenues owed the Palestinians, end house and road demolitions, and take other measures to protect Palestinian civilians, including the prevention of settler violence.

The Report did not, however, meet the Palestinian demand that Israel return its troops to the positions held on 28 September 2000, the day the Intifada broke out. The recommendation was only that Israel should "consider" such a move.

There were demands upon the Palestinians as well. While illegal arms were to be prohibited and other measures taken to deal with Palestinian violence, the most important demands involved the need to organize the Palestinian security forces in order to provide a clear chain of command, accountability and a code of conduct.

The final recommendation called for the resumption of negotiations. Actually throughout the Report and in the various recommendations, the Committee reiterated its conviction that neither an end to violence nor confidence-building measures was sustainable if negotiations were deferred. The report explicitly avoided suggestions regarding the substance of such negotiations, making do with a recommendation that they be held in the spirit of compromise, reconciliation and partnership.

The emphasis on the need to resume negotiations was an indirect negation of the "no partner" stance of Israel, but perhaps still more importantly, the recommendations neither stated nor implied conditionality. The only sequentiality was first the 100% effort by both sides to end the violence, that is, the ceasefire, to be followed immediately by the confidence-building measures, which Israel and the Palestinians were to undertake simultaneously, together with resuming negotiations.

Israel's interpretation of the recommendations was apparent in its official acceptance of the Report.[2] It noted its agreement with the call for cessation of the violence and resumption of negotiations, ignoring the title given the middle set of recommendations, namely Rebuilding of Confidence, and instead inserted the first recommendation in that section, namely, the need for a cooling-off period. Both officially and in subsequent behavior, Israel agreed to not only the ceasefire but also the cooling-off period as conditions for moving forward, and it defined these as the complete end of Palestinian violence and terrorism along with implementation of all the security tasks recommended for the Palestinian side. The Israeli steps, though not officially mentioned, were presumably to come only after all this, along with negotiations. Thus Israel substituted its own definition of the Report's references to a Palestinian "100% effort" and virtually ignored the commitments demanded of Israel (explicitly ruling out the recommendations regarding the settlements), while it added a sequentiality that most likely was not intended by the Mitchell Committee.

The Palestinians, for their part, accepted the Report without reservation, adding many more demands regarding measures Israel should take.[3] However, the key to the Palestinian response was its acceptance of the Report as a whole and its call for immediate implementation of the recommendations "as a comprehensive package." Further, the Palestinians especially noted the role of the international community, seizing upon the discussion (but not recommendation) for an international protection force as a measure that should be reconsidered. The Palestinians' official response to the report provided a relatively detailed call for third party involvement to supervise and ensure implementation of the recommendations. The use of TIPH for this purpose, as suggested by the Report, would have to be accompanied by a new mandate for the group so that it might effectively stop abuses of international law (already listed under Israel's abuses of international law).

It was natural that each side would interpret the Report according to its own interests, and in fact neither side did anything to implement even the first recommendation. The Israeli implicit and explicit addition of conditionality and sequentiality evolved into the doctrine of refusing to negotiate under fire, accompanied by a broad definition that included everything the Palestinians were supposed to do in order to rebuild confidence and before Israel would act or resume negotiations.

Since nothing was done to implement the Mitchell Committee recommendations, and the violence continued with increasing intensity, the Americans, in the form of the head of the CIA, George Tenet, proposed a Cease-fire Plan.[4] To counter or accommodate Israel's sequential interpretation that stalled the implementation of the recommendations, The Tenet Plan telescoped the first two stages recommended by the Mitchell Committee. Thus, Tenet's so-called Cease-fire Plan actually contained not only the declaration of a ceasefire and resumption of security cooperation of the "End the Violence" section of the Mitchell recommendations, but also included virtually all the security-related measures called for in the second "Rebuild Confidence" section. In addition, there were also quite detailed security steps to be followed by both sides for cooperation and smooth implementation.

The Tenet plan called for a joint Palestinian-Israeli-American security committee to resolve all issues connected with implementation of the Plan. It also called for "demonstrable" achievements of various measures, accompanied by a timetable for some of the specific steps to be taken by both sides. The major innovation, for the Palestinians' sake, was the declared objective of restoring the situation that had existed on the ground prior to 28 September (the beginning of the Intifada) including a timetable to be determined by the security committee for the redeployment of Israeli troops to the positions held on 28 September 2000. Also to the Palestinians' liking, the Tenet Plan stated that "untoward events" should not be permitted to disrupt the security cooperation—a clause that provided a means for getting around Israel's conditionality and promised to eliminate the past and frequent problem of terror attacks bringing all progress to a halt.

Almost a year later, on 26 March 2002, with still no ceasefire, American envoy General (ret.) Anthony Zinni issued a very similar proposal with detailed steps for both sides along with a short timetable of approximately four weeks for implementation. While Zinni's proposal added still more detailed security measures for both sides, and was interpreted to be a plan for implementing the Tenet Plan, it deviated from the Tenet Plan in a few ways. Some of these ways were considered quite important by the Palestinians. Zinni called for Israeli redeployment to the 28 September 2001 lines, but his proposals were more vague than Tenet's as to when the timetable for this redeployment would be set (in Tenet's plan the redeployment schedule was to have been set within the first week of the resumption of security cooperation and even begun while the schedule was being determined). For the Palestinians this was not a minor difference since Israeli withdrawal to the September 2000 lines was their most urgent concern, involving also the lifting of checkpoints and closures within the West Bank, areas theoretically under PA jurisdiction. Zinni's plan was problematic for the Palestinians also in the fact that it did not cancel Israel's conditionality, that is, Zinni's plan did not contain Tenet's clause about the need to continue cooperation even in case of "untoward events." Further, a purely security oriented document, the Zinni proposal made no mention whatsoever of the Mitchell Report, even as the context for the proposal. The Palestinians complained about this lacuna, preferring the Tenet Plan, which had been viewed as a means for enabling progress to the rest of the Mitchell Committee recommendations on non-security measures connected with the occupation (settlements, for example) and negotiations.

Neither the Tenet nor the Zinni proposals had a verification mechanism beyond the existence of the joint security committee (US, PA and Israel). The Palestinians claimed that the original version of the Zinni proposals had at least accorded this group responsibility for monitoring and verification, but the proposal that reached the public (and apparently the final proposal presented to the two sides) spoke only of "assessing" progress at each stage of the security measures.[5] The Palestinians clearly preferred the Tenet Plan, but neither plan was in fact implemented. As had become usual, there was no agreement as to which should come first—end of terror or beginning of Israeli withdrawal from post 28 September 2000 positions—in addition to the disagreements over scheduling and the opening of negotiations. Basically, Israel was unwilling to move forward in any way until terrorism was halted entirely and what it called the "terror infrastructure" was demolished. No ceasefire ensued; the violence continued, taking an unprecedented toll on both sides, with no end or negotiations in sight.

CHAPTER SEVEN

The Saudi Initiative-Arab League Resolution and UNSC Resolution 1397

Even as the parties to the conflict were mulling over Zinni's proposals, the international community, including the Arab world, sought greater involvement. Saudi Arabia stepped dramatically into the picture with a peace initiative put forth by Crown Prince Abdullah, which was ultimately adopted by the Arab League on 28 March 2002.[1] The Crown Prince offered "the establishment of normal relations with Israel in the context of a comprehensive peace" in exchange for Israeli withdrawal from the territories occupied since 1967, implementation of Resolution 242 on the basis of the principle of land for peace, and Israeli acceptance of the creation of a Palestinian state with the capital in East Jerusalem. Like Sadat in 1977, the Saudis understood the key to Israeli fears: the promise of normalization, acceptance of Israel into the region.

The Arab League summit held in Beirut a few weeks after the Saudi initiative, and attended by all twenty-two Arab states, reiterated the Saudi proposal with one important addition.[2] This concerned the sensitive issue of the refugees, but the formulation was new and promising. The article read: "Achievement of a just solution to the Palestinian refugee problem to be agreed upon in accordance with UNGA resolution 194." Thus, although there was explicit reference to Resolution 194, the right of return as such was not stated. Still more importantly, the "just solution" was to be "agreed upon." Such a formulation implied the need for Israeli agreement, thereby softening the demand, and in keeping with many of the Palestinian explanations regarding implementation, it provided a way for Israel to protect its interests. The interests of Arab states were also taken into consideration in a clause that permitted Arab host states to reject "patriation" that conflicted with the "special circumstances" of these states—the reference probably being to Jordan given its already large Palestinian population, although Lebanon too may have been intended. Thus the principle that limitations might be placed on numbers of refugees to be settled in a given Arab state, and the principle of Israeli agreement with regard to its policy, were accepted. Together with the express willingness to normalize relations with Israel, these innovations were most significant, providing what might be a basis—now agreed by the Arab world—for resolving the conflict.

Israeli reaction to the Saudi initiative had been skeptical at best, but once the Arab League added the refugee clause with the specific reference to Resolution 194, the government had no problem ignoring the initiative altogether. Moreover, no government in Israel had ever publicly agreed to the 1967 lines, even though Barak and Rabin before him had referred to these lines as a framework of sorts. In fact the Arab initiative was virtually forgotten by the Israeli press and public in the wake of the particularly horrific terrorist attack on Passover Seder celebrants at a hotel in northern Israel, killing 30 Israeli civilians, followed by the retaliatory Israeli invasion of Palestinian areas in the West Bank. The terrorist attack, culminating a series of attacks throughout the month, occurred just one day before the Beirut Arab League summit; the invasion occurred just a few days after the meeting. Both events thrust the initiative into near oblivion. This was most regrettable inasmuch as the Arab League version of the initiative provided at least a basis for an agreement.[3] Obviously this was not a detailed peace plan; the difficult issues of exact borders and especially that of Jerusalem required continuation of the talks halted at Taba. But the offer of normalization combined with the new Arab League-approved compromise formula for resolution of the sensitive refugee issue, both intended to get Israel back to the negotiating table, could—one might say, should—have changed the entire course of events in the region.

Almost unnoticed in the midst of the violence and all the proposals floating around at the time, the UN Security Council adopted a resolution affirming the idea of a Palestinian state for the first time. The resolution came in response to the violence, but its first clause recalled Resolutions 242 and 338 (which had not included Palestinian national rights in any form) and its second clause affirmed "a vision of a region where two states, Israel and Palestine, live side by side within secure and recognized borders." The resolution dealt mainly with a call for an end to the violence and the implementation of the Mitchell and Tenet recommendations. However, this preamble now added the missing link in the chain of resolutions concerning the Arab-Israeli conflict: Resolution 181 (1947) which had called for the partition of Palestine into a Jewish and an Arab state; Resolution 194 (1948) which dealt with the internationalization of Jerusalem and repatriation of the refugees; Resolution 242 (1967) which called for Israeli withdrawal from territories taken in 1967 and recognition of all states in the area, including Israel's right to live in secure and recognized borders; Resolution 338 (1973) ending the Yom Kippur War and calling for negotiations for peace. Now Resolution 1397 allowed for the creation of a Palestinian state in addition to the State of Israel. In approving this resolution, the United States was for the first time, albeit indirectly, accepting the idea of a Palestinian state.[4]

CHAPTER EIGHT

President Bush: October 2001—
The Rose Garden Speech June 2002

George W. Bush had initially refrained from the kind of direct and intensive American involvement characteristic of the Clinton administration. Generally he had made do with the dispatch of envoys such as Tenet and Zinni. Following 9/11 (September 2001), however, he took a somewhat deeper interest, viewing the conflict from the perspective of his war on terror. Within this context, Bush tended to see Sharon as an ally and Arafat as the terrorist, and he gradually applied his "regime-change/democratic reform" concepts to the Palestinian situation. Nonetheless, even as he criticized Arafat and eventually (June 2002) called for the Palestinians to choose a new leader, he was the first US President to publicly endorse the creation of a Palestinian state. As President, Clinton had done so only in talks and proposals presented to the two sides, but never made a public, much less an official, declaration to that effect.

Bush made his pronouncement for the first time almost off-handedly in a press conference following a meeting with Congressional leaders on 2 October 2001.[1] In answer to a direct question, Bush said "a Palestinian State has always been part of a vision, so long as the right to Israel to exist is respected."

Evidence that this was not just a slip of the tongue came when the president repeated the statement, albeit after Sharon had made a similar comment on 7 February 2002 in a press conference held by the two leaders.[2] Then Bush said again that a Palestinian state was "an ultimate aim" supported by the United States.[3] While he said the Palestinians must end terrorism and implement the Mitchell Committee recommendations, it was not until his 24 June 2002 Rose Garden speech, however, that Bush added any substance to the idea publicly.

Bush was willing to speak in any detail only about a "provisional Pales- tinian State" to be created after the Palestinians had "new leaders and new institutions." The borders would be provisional, to be determined by the final settlement, along with the status of Jerusalem, the refugee issue and "other aspects of sovereignty." The final settlement was to be based on Resolutions 242 and 338 and an end of the Israeli occupation. But this in no way clarified the border issue since there were quite a few varied interpretations as to just what territories were meant by the resolutions. The most Bush was to say was that the Palestinian state that would emerge in the end would have to be "viable and credible." The implication presumably was that cantonization or lack of territorial contiguity would not be acceptable. The timeframe to reach this final status would be three years.

Prior to the final status negotiations, there were a number of steps that Bush demanded. To get to the provisional state, the Palestinian authority was to undertake total political, economic and security reform. Such reforms were to produce a constitution, separation of powers, an independent judiciary, rule of law, a working legislature, authoritative local and government officials, multiparty local and national elections, a market economy, action against ter- rorism and against corruption, plus a security system with a unified chain of command, clear lines of authority and accountability. Thus the Palestine Authority was to become an American-modeled society as a condition for creation of the provisional state.

While theoretically it might indeed be desirable to have a western-style democracy in Palestine, Bush was in effect adding a demand that was not ger- mane to the conflict. In fact, it was one that might seriously complicate, even impede, an agreement. The demand for a western-style democracy clearly reflected the US Administration's new foreign policy, but it also inadvertently

assumed one of the more hard-line demands of the Israeli right-wing, originally raised by Netanyahu, that had had the main purpose of putting off
any need for Israeli compromise until the possibly unlikely advent of Palestinian democracy. The claim by Netanyahu and later Natan Sharansky was
that peace could only be made with a democracy (an erroneous extrapolation
from the theory that democracies do not fight democracies), overlooking the
fact that Israel had made peace with both Jordan and Egypt, and that many
conflicts in the world had been resolved in peace agreements between non-
democratic partners.

During this preliminary period, according to Bush Israel was to undertake the measures outlined in the Mitchell recommendations regarding freedom of movement and employment in Israel for the Palestinians, along with
the transfer of owed tax revenues to "honest, accountable hands," i.e., not to
the corrupt PA or Arafat. In keeping with Mitchell, though conditional on the
reduction of violence, Israel was to halt settlement activity and withdraw to
the lines of 28 September 2000. Both in the details and in repeated comments,
Bush basically accepted Israel's conditionality of reduced violence and Palestinian action again terrorism and the elimination of its infrastructure prior to
even moving to a provisional state or negotiations.

Bush made some references to third parties, though not the international
presence or protection forces raised at Camp David and in the Clinton parameters. Instead, outside assistance was suggested for the Palestinians, both
for economic matters and the designing of a plan for the reforms. Outside
supervision was demanded, not just suggested, for the rebuilding of the security services, much the way this had been required as early as the Wye
Memorandum. Thus Bush continued the Israeli right-wing's interpretation of
international involvement only as a check on the Palestinians.

The only comfort the Palestinians might have found in Bush's statement
were the references to the need to end the occupation and the goal of creating
a viable and credible Palestinian state, theoretically within three years. This
was no small point; the delineation of three years finally made the goal clear
within a particular, relatively short, timeframe. However, all this was conditional upon the Palestinians doing everything demanded for the creation first
of a "provisional state." One could certainly see the influence of Bush's overall

plan for democratization of the Middle East, now applied to the Palestinian Authority, and the idea of regime change applied to Arafat, along with the American president's preoccupation with the war on terror, also applied to the Palestinian Authority. This suited not only Sharon's interests in putting off any moves until Palestinian terror was stamped out, but also his interest in avoiding negotiations indefinitely—since the conditionality belied Bush's stated timetable of three years. Thus, this "vision" was a far cry from an actual peace plan or the basis for a peace plan such as Clinton's Parameters; nor was it even a logical outline of steps toward negotiations as recommended by the Mitchell Committee. What Bush presented in the Rose Garden, however, was basically the American understanding of the Road Map that was soon to be presented by the international community acting through a quartet.

CHAPTER NINE

The Road Map—30 April 2003

The Quartet, consisting of the United Nations, the European Union, the United States and Russia, met throughout the second half of 2002, and on 30 April officially presented a plan explicitly said to be based on Bush's Rose Garden speech.[1] The Preamble stated the goal of reaching a negotiated settlement of the Israeli-Palestinian conflict and an end of the occupation that began in 1967, invoking all the relevant resolutions (242, 338) including the newer Resolution 1397 and even the Arab League Resolution as the bases for the settlement. The designation of 1967 in reference to the occupation was designed to clarify that Palestinian land before 1948 was no longer an issue, that is, that the territorial conflict would be resolved once the 1967 occupation ended. Resolutions 242 and 338 provided recognition of Israel, necessitating mention of Resolution 1397 and the Arab League Resolution in order to add Palestinian statehood, which was missing from previous resolutions.[2] While these were the bases for the settlement to be negotiated, it was also explicitly stated that the settlement would result in the emergence of a Palestinian state (reflecting Bush's preferences, this was now characterized as an "independent, democratic and viable state"), as well as an end to the conflict.

The latter was of course Israel's main interest. The Arab League Resolution was especially noted for its value in also resolving the Syrian and Lebanese conflicts with Israel.

The preamble and title indicated that the Road Map was a "performance-based" plan, based on reciprocal steps, with progress explicitly tied to performance by each side of its obligations. Yet at the outset it also stated that the plan had "clear phases, timelines, target dates and benchmarks," to encompass a period of three years ending in 2005. It was not clear just how the target dates and benchmarks were to be met and the timeline fulfilled if the sides did not perform as demanded, since it was explicitly stated that "non-compliance with obligations will impede progress." This inherent, and critical, contradiction was not explained, although it obviously was intended to satisfy both the Palestinians' interest in a clear deadline for creation of their state and the Israelis' insistence upon conditionality every step of the way. Moreover, conditionality seemed to contradict the final statement of the preamble that the parties were "to perform their obligations *in parallel* [emphasis mine] unless otherwise indicated," despite the earlier characterization of the steps as "reciprocal."

Phase I ("present to May 2003")[3] of the Road Map was basically to be implementation of the Tenet Plan and Mitchell Committee recommendations with additional demands dictated by Bush's vision of a democratic Palestine. The very first measures were to be declarations by each side. Basically the Palestinians were to reiterate their declaration (contained in the Oslo Accords) regarding Israel's right to exist and call for an immediate ceasefire. Israel was also to call for an immediate ceasefire and declare its commitment to the creation of a Palestinian state. These and the following Palestinian and Israeli measures were to be simultaneous (or parallel), although some steps would logically have to be sequential. The only measure actually said to be conditional was Israeli withdrawal to the 28 September 2000 lines, which was to begin "as comprehensive security performance moves forward." The subtitles within the first phase, however, suggested a time sequence regarding humanitarian steps Israel was to take, which is discussed below.

The "security performance" referred to above consisted of many demands primarily connected with Palestinian action against violence and terrorism, including the dismantling of the terrorist infrastructure and confiscation of illegal weapons. The numerous Palestinian security organizations were to be consolidated into three units and subordinated to one authority, the Ministry of Interior. Security cooperation would be resumed with Israel, and Israel was called upon specifically to refrain from actions that might undermine trust, such as deportations, attacks on civilians, demolition or confiscation of Palestinian institutions or property (for punitive or construction purposes), and various other measures said to be specified in the Tenet Plan.

At the same time, a detailed program under the subtitle of Palestinian institution-building was to take place, including the drafting of a constitution and the selection of an interim prime minister and ministers, to be followed by selection of an elections committee, an election law and the holding of elections. Each of these steps, many of which were logically sequential, was described in some detail specifying such things as separation of powers, multiparty election campaign with open debate and transparent candidate selection, and other such prescriptions. Moreover, there was a demand for economic, administrative and judicial reforms as determined by an International Task Force on Palestinian Reform.[4] Israel for its part was to facilitate travel for Palestinians in connection with official or reform-related work, as well as facilitate the assistance given from outside for the election process. Israel was also to facilitate voter registration, movement of candidates and voting officials. Of a more substantive nature, Israel was to permit the reopening of Palestinian institutions that had been closed in East Jerusalem provided they operated in accord with previous agreements, meaning presumably the Oslo Accords barring Palestine Authority activity in East Jerusalem.

The next subtitle within Phase I was "Humanitarian Response," wording which was misleading for it suggested that humanitarian measures were to come only in response to measures in the previous security and institution-building sections of the Road Map. However, sequentiality seems unintended, for these measures included such critical undertakings as the donor-assisted effort for economic development and the reforms. Presumably assistance of this type would occur at the same time as the reforms. Under the same heading, Israel was to improve the humanitarian situation in the occupied territories including lifting curfews, easing restrictions on the movement of persons and goods and allowing unfettered access for international and humanitarian personnel. Rather than list further humanitarian measures, the Road Map called for full implementation of all the recommendations in the Bertini Report. This was a lengthy and highly critical (mainly of Israel) UN-sponsored study that called on Israel to undertake a relatively long list of measures for the welfare of the Palestinians in the areas of education, health, sanitation and water, security, the economy and more.[5] Since many of the humanitarian measures, particularly those connected with freedom of movement, could be considered prerequisites for elections and other democratic procedures previously demanded in Phase I, they would logically occur simultaneously rather than sequentially. In addition, Israel was to continue the transfer of revenues and funds according to an agreed monitoring mechanism.

The matter of simultaneous versus sequential movement through the Road Map was neither a minor point nor a question of phrasing. By subsequently interpreting these and other steps as sequential, Israel in effect created conditions (and obstacles) where the authors of the Road Map may not have intended them.

The next section was subtitled Civil Society, which called for continued donor support and civil society initiatives along with private sector development. And the last section dealt with settlements. Israel was to "immediately" dismantle outposts erected since March 2001, namely the unauthorized (officially) settlement outposts erected in the period since Sharon formed his government. The outposts, as they were called, were in fact small temporary settlements, often consisting of just a few trailers, intended to lay stake to an area, without official authorization or planning, for the construction of a future settlement. These were often but not necessarily in the vicinity of already existing settlements. The outpost campaign began at the time of the Wye Memorandum when Sharon, then Foreign Minister, publicly told the settlers to grab every hill and piece of land possible, presumably before the Wye Memorandum went into effect.[6] Shortly after the election of Barak, Israeli peace activists (Peace Now's Settlement Watch) discovered these outposts and brought the issue to public attention. The "illegal outposts" as the government now called them, which in fact were no more or less illegal according to international law than all the settlements regardless of Israeli government authorization, were nothing more than the nuclei of new settlements designed to circumvent international and American demands for a freeze on settlement building. Thus they were treated more severely in the Road Map, which also demanded, as part of Phase I, a freeze on all settlement activity including natural growth, in accord with the Mitchell Committee Report.

There was also to be a certain amount of outside involvement, in various forms, as part of Phase I. For example, major donor assistance was referred to, with the condition that such assistance, in particular budgetary assistance, was to be channeled through a single Palestinian treasury account. This detail had the obvious purpose of eliminating the corruption that had set in particularly with regard to donor funds. A different kind of international involvement was that of the International Task Force on Palestinian Reform that was to provide plans for reform and assistance with the Palestinian elections. In the security realm, aside from the demand that Arab states halt all aid to groups supporting or engaged in violence or terrorism, there was to be an "oversight board" consisting of the United States, Egypt and Jordan to collaborate in the American training, rebuilding and resuming of security cooperation. Exactly what role Egypt and Jordan were to have was unclear; an American role in the security area had been agreed as early as the Wye Memorandum, although the Road Map appeared to provide the United States a broader role. In addition, a vague reference to the Quartet support for "efforts to achieve" a ceasefire was included.

However, the most important international involvement was the provision for some kind of outside monitoring. The preamble to the Road Map had said that the Quartet would meet regularly to evaluate performance and implementation, and this was elaborated upon slightly in the security measures of Phase I. A monitoring mechanism, so regrettably missing from the Oslo Accords and from Mitchell and Tenet as well, was finally proposed. During Phase I, representatives of the Quartet were to conduct informal monitoring using "existing mechanisms and on-the-ground resources." At the same time, they were to begin consultations for the establishment of a formal monitoring mechanism and its operation. This important matter was apparently put this way because the Road Map was to be put into immediate effect with relatively short timelines, which presumably meant there was no time to open with a formal monitoring mechanism in place.

Phase II ("June 2003–December 2003") was to begin once the Quartet determined, by consensus, that conditions were "appropriate to proceed," based on the performance of the two parties. More specifically, this phase was to begin after the Palestinian elections and end with the establishment of the Palestinian state in provisional borders. This phase was basically designated as a period of transition for the completion and consolidation of the measures introduced in the first phase. The Palestinians were to finalize and ratify their constitution, followed by formally empowering a cabinet and a prime minister. Nothing was said specifically about the powers of the prime minister, but in keeping with Bush's call for the replacement of Arafat, there were, at this time, international efforts to have the Palestinians create the position of prime minister with enough power to counter if not actually replace Arafat (who held the elected position of President of the Palestinian Authority). The security performance called for in Phase I was to continue, including in particular "effective security cooperation." There was to be continued normalization of the Palestinians' lives, along with the building of their institutions, but no specific measures were included in this connection.

All of the above processes or measures were to be launched by an international conference, which would also deal with Palestinian economic development. However, the international conference was apparently to have still broader objectives, for the Road Map described it as "inclusive" so as to have the purpose of achieving a comprehensive peace between Israel and Syria and Lebanon as well. Apparently, as part of this effort, the other Arab states were to resume the relations they had with Israel prior to the al-Aksa Intifada (such as trade offices and interest sections), and the multilateral talks begun in the pre-Oslo period (as a result of the 1991 Madrid conference) were to be reopened. As in the past, the multilaterals would deal with the issues of water, environment, economic development, refugees, and arms control.

Thus, the international role was much larger in this second phase, primarily in the form of the International Conference. In addition, the Quartet committed itself to promoting international recognition of the Palestinian state (with its provisional borders) even to the point of UN membership. At this stage, as in Phase I, the most important international involvement may well have been the promised monitoring mechanism. All that was said in this regard, however, was that there would be an "enhanced" international role in the monitoring of this period, with the "active, sustained and operational support of the Quartet." One could only assume that this would mean an actual monitoring mechanism on the ground however it might be designed during the previous phase.

Little was said about the Palestinian state itself, aside from the provisional nature of its borders and its characterization as independent and democratic. These were apparently to be determined in Israeli-Palestinian negotiations launched by the International Conference. The Road Map did state that previous (unspecified) agreements were to be implemented to enhance "maximum" territorial contiguity. These were to include what the document called "further action on the settlements in conjunction with the creation of the Palestinian state." This was in fact one of the most incomprehensible clauses in the Road Map, although the presumed meaning was that the degree of territorial contiguity would be determined by the size and location of the remaining Jewish settlements.

Phase III ("2004–2005") was (optimistically) entitled "Permanent Status Agreement and End of the Israeli-Palestinian Conflict." It was to begin similarly as Phase II, once the Quartet agreed by consensus that the parties were ready to progress to the next phase, based not only on the parties' actions but also, this time, the monitoring conducted by the Quartet. As in Phase II, this period was to see a continuation of Palestinian institution-building, reform measures and security performance and the cooperation of the previous phases, all in preparation for a final status agreement. There was to be international assistance in these efforts, together with help in stabilizing the Palestinian economy.

The most important international role in Phase III, however, was to be the convening of another International Conference at the beginning of 2004. The first task of the conference would be to endorse the agreement reached on the establishment of the Palestinian state with provisional borders—although in fact this state was already to have been created by the end of the

Phase II and the Quartet was supposed to have already begun seeking recognition and UN membership for it. This done, the conference would launch the process, namely Israeli-Palestinian negotiations, leading to a final, permanent status agreement in 2005. The Quartet was to provide this process with "active, sustained and operational" support, although this received no further amplification or explanation in the text. The Quartet would also support an effort to reach, "as soon as possible," a comprehensive Middle East peace settlement between Israel, Lebanon and Syria—efforts apparently begun at the first International Conference in Phase II.

The guidelines or parameters for the final status agreement with the Palestinians were laid out only in a general form. Of course the agreement was to be based on Resolutions 242 and 338, along with 1397 as stated in the preamble of the Road Map, and ending the occupation that began in 1967, also as stated in the preamble. This was the extent to which the border issue was addressed, with no reference to contiguity or settlements, though they were mentioned in the earlier phases. And there was also a reference to viability in the call for a two-state solution between Israel and a "sovereign, independent, democratic, and viable Palestine."

With regard to the refugees, the solution was somewhat different from the Arab League Resolution. It avoided mention of Resolution 194 (because of Israeli sensitivities) but calling for an "agreed, just, fair and realistic solution." This is the first time the word "realistic" appeared in an official peace proposal. It too was presumably there for the sake of Israeli interests, but it is not clear how a "realistic" solution could also be a "just" solution. However, the key concept was contained in the word "agreed," which had been the important contribution of the Arab League Resolution on this issue. The principles laid out for resolution of the Jerusalem issue referred only generally to the need to take into account the political and religious concerns of both sides, and protect the religious interests of Jews, Christians and Muslims worldwide.

The final agreement was also to fulfill the vision of the two states living side by side in peace and security. The Arab League promise of full, normal relations with Israel and security for all states in the region was to be implemented.

▪ A Critical View of the Road Map

Since the Road Map was the only document officially accepted after Oslo by the parties concerned (Israel's reservations will be discussed below), and since it may still provide the guidelines in one form or another for peacemaking in the near future, it is important to understand the flaws in the document. On the whole, the Road Map was characterized by vagueness and in some places even contradictions, but there were more important substantive and conceptual problems. It was once again, like the Oslo Accords, a phased, basically interim agreement designed to create certain processes that would ultimately lead to still more processes that would in the end determine the final status of the occupied territories and the relationship between Israel and Palestine. More than the purely security oriented Tenet Plan, less than the more balanced Mitchell Committee Recommendations, the Road Map did, at least, add something to the Oslo Accords in that it provided for the creation of a Palestinian state, albeit a state with only provisional borders.

Nonetheless, the Road Map was yet another set of complicated procedures and measures, creating once again a period of time, albeit shorter than the three years of Oslo, until negotiations on a final status agreement would even begin. The major problem with this was that once again there would be "testing" of the two sides, in this case actually as a basis for the plan. And this "testing" could well delay or suspend the prescribed steps and procedures. Moreover, during these periods of "testing," opponents to the successful conclusion of any agreement could disrupt the entire process, as previously was the case. While an outline for immediate steps to resume negotiations was needed (and existed in both the Tenet Plan and Mitchell Committee Report), the creation once again of a prolonged process was conceptually flawed—unless, of course, the purpose was to postpone any real resolution of the conflict. It is doubtful that this was the intention of the European Union, the Russians, or the UN, but it is conceivable that the United States was interested primarily in the appearance of some kind of process and relative stability (especially in view of the Iraqi crisis), rather than actual difficult, possibly frustrating and unsuccessful, Israeli-Palestinian negotiations for a final peace agreement.

The authors of the Road Map apparently sought to cope with the flaws of the Oslo Accords and subsequent plans, specifically with regard to the problems of the transition period. The announcement from the outset that there would be a Palestinian state and the actual creation of such a state, albeit with provisional borders, at the end of the second phase were designed to provide an incentive for the Palestinians to adhere to the various demands in the Road Map. The provision of assurances as to where the Map was ultimately leading was vital, given the past disappointments and deeply ingrained skepticism on the part of the Palestinians. The counterpart for Israel was the demand that as early as the first stage of Phase I the Palestinians issue an "unequivocal statement reiterating Israel's right to exist in peace and security." This was indeed required in view of the conviction that had grown amongst the Israeli public that the purpose of the al-Aksa Intifada had not been to end the occupation but rather to destroy the state of Israel.

However, the promise of statehood was more than a confidence-building measure since it was part of the basis for negotiations provided by the Quartet (as well as by Mitchell and by Bush's Rose Garden speech). Yet, first the Palestinians were going to have to pass through the stage of a state with provisional borders. The idea of a state with only provisional borders was an unusual one, although in a sense Israel is such a state since its final borders have yet to be defined or recognized internationally. It is exactly this example that the Palestinians would fear, since the "provisional border" might well turn into something far more long-term, as did the armistice lines for Israel until 1967 and as the ceasefire lines on the West Bank and Golan Heights did from then onward, until this day. More to the point, there was also the possibility that the idea of a provisional border, whether intentionally or unintentionally, might simply be a device to create what may have been Sharon's idea of a Palestinian state in the present areas A and B or the roughly forty-two percent of the West Bank of which he had spoken in the past. The Road Map did not foresee the prolongation of this provisional border since negotiations were meant to take place in Phase III regarding a permanent border. Nonetheless, Palestinian concerns were expressed to the effect that three years from then (or whenever the Road Map were finally initiated) and possibly many years longer, they would find themselves in exactly the same position they were in when the Oslo process collapsed, namely ruling over a limited area surrounded and intersected by Israeli forces, with negotiations for a final border delayed, suspended, or indefinitely drawn-out.

Herein, again, was the problem of interim agreements, when in fact negotiations regarding final borders had been held long before and almost reached conclusion in Taba. The Road Map implied that there would be (pre) negotiations even for the provisional borders before Phase II actually approved them. Conceivably this could be avoided by the Israeli withdrawal to the 28 September 2000 lines which was allowed conditionally in Phase I. Since the publication of the Road Map, a fence and walls (separation barrier) have been erected by Israel, which could serve as the "provisional border" envisaged by the Road Map, better perhaps than the pre-Intifada lines (Oslo II areas) but still not the 1967 lines.[7] In any case, there was little reason once again to put off finalization of the borders and even the negotiations for final borders, pending all the other steps outlined by the Quartet, for still another two or three years of uncertainty. Indeed the Palestinians had argued that Israel would simply exploit this new interim period to create more "facts on the ground," namely settlements, outposts, and by-pass roads, reducing still further the land available for the Palestinian state, and in defiance of the Road Map's reiteration of the need to freeze settlement activity.

The introduction of a monitoring mechanism was also meant to remedy a lacuna in the Oslo Accords. If, however, the Quartet believed such a body was necessary, it is not clear why it was not to be introduced fully and formally in Phase I. Indeed Phase I was perhaps the period in which monitoring would be most needed since it would be the phase in which the measures against violence and terrorism were to be implemented, the ceasefire ensured, the Palestinian institutions built and confidence, meaning trust, be restored between the two sides after the traumatic events of the past few years. If these tasks were achieved in Phase I as assumed by the Road Map, then monitoring in the subsequent phases would be much easier and less critical. Nor is it clear just what was meant by "on the ground resources" or "informal" monitoring. Who and upon what authority would the monitoring take place; how would the monitors operate, what would their mandate be? While they were to be assigned the task of providing the Quartet with the information necessary to determine "performance"—the condition for moving from Phase to Phase—it is not clear how the monitoring group would do this or if it would also have additional tasks. For example, would it monitor or arbitrate disputes on a daily basis, would it have any authority with respect to the two sides to the conflict or would it serve merely as a reporting body to the Quartet? More concretely, in case of violence or actions on the ground, would the monitors have any authority (or capability) to intervene? And if the powers of the monitoring group were limited to determining the "ripeness" for progressing from phase to phase, any one party, by virtue of its veto power, could delay movement forward. Given Israel's traditional opposition to third-party involvement, Jerusalem would presumably prefer greatly limiting the jurisdiction and authority of the monitors, while the Palestinians favored expansion even to the point of introducing international forces to guide the entire process.[8] Surprisingly, the "review of international support mechanisms" for the Road Map conducted by the international community at a follow-up meeting in March 2005 in London did not deal with the these problems at all, limiting its discussions to what it called supporting the Palestinian Authority.[9]

In keeping with Washington's demand for democratization of the Arab world, much of the first phase and almost all of the second phase were dedicated to a reconstruction of the Palestinian Authority down to the details of devolving authority to local bodies and up to the writing of a constitution (it should be noted that Israel does not have a written constitution or balance of powers, but the Road Map did not make such demands on Israel). These and other steps were also designed at the time to eliminate the authority of Arafat, as desired by Israel and supported by the United States. In fact these clauses of the Road Map generally coincided with the conditions laid down by Sharon for a return to negotiations (pronounced at the Herzliya Conference in early December 2002 while the Road Map was still being drawn up): absolute cessation of terror, violence and incitement on the Palestinian side; implementation of fundamental reforms in the Palestinian Authority including the removal of Arafat's authority; establishment of a new Palestinian Authority that would operate with accountability and dismantle the terror infrastructure; and finally free elections. The Palestinians themselves had begun to move toward reform and democratization at the time, but it would be most surprising if they were to accept the mini-management of this process as outlined in the Road Map and, particularly, the undemocratic interference in Palestinian political life by demanding appointment of a prime minister, which meant the virtual replacement of Arafat without elections (the Road Map called for elections only of a new legislative council). This appointment was ultimately forced upon the Palestinians, even without formal commencement of the Road Map. But it was a measure that would become still more problematic and ironic when, after Arafat's death, a new president, Abu Mazen (Mahmoud Abbas), was elected—a leader welcomed by Washington who would prefer to weaken the position of prime minister.

The provision of a timetable in the Road Map was of great importance if one were anxious to return to negotiations and reach a final settlement. Yet even the three-year interim period outlined by the Road Map timetable was not fixed since progress from one phase to another was dependant upon "performance." How the monitors would interpret performance and with what authority their judgments would be issued was totally unclear and important, particularly given the possibility that extremist forces on either side could well ensure "non-performance." The final assessment of progress and readiness to move forward rested with the Quartet itself, but the criteria for their judgment of performance were no less ambiguous. These were crucial problems that might cripple implementation of the Road Map to the point of totally destroying the process altogether. Moreover, far from clearing up the problem of sequentiality versus simultaneous implementation that plagued the Mitchell Committee recommendations, the Road Map added to the ambiguity by speaking of "reciprocal" steps, conducted "in parallel" but conditional for moving from phase to phase (and in the case of Israeli withdrawal to the 28 September lines, explicitly sequential and conditional). Sharon had exploited such ambiguity in the past in order to put off negotiations; the Road Map might not prevent the same from recurring in the future.

Thus both the conceptual and concrete problems with the Road Map were most likely the result of an effort to square the circle, namely to respond to the demands of both the Palestinian Authority and the Israeli government, each with the unofficial backing of the Europeans and Americans respectively. It would appear that the more times this attempt was made, the greater the demands and the more complicated the resultant plans. The Israeli-Palestinian conflict was not the first conflict to suffer from unnecessary (and tragic) prolongation because of ever increasing and complicated pre-conditions for negotiations. The various parties concerned undoubtedly believed that such pre-conditions were far from arbitrary, but experience has shown that many lives have been needlessly lost because of an unwillingness of the parties concerned to cut their losses on the battlefield, so to speak, and proceed with haste to negotiate a settlement. The Road Map did not appear to have benefited from such experience.

Although officially accepting the Road Map, Israel submitted to the Americans a list of fourteen reservations, some of them of a nature that could significantly cripple implementation of the plan.[10] Perhaps the most problematic were the demands that the declarations opening Phase I include a reference to Israel's right to exist as a Jewish state and a "waiver of any right of return for Palestinian refugees to the state of Israel." The demand to foreclose the refugee issue even before final status talks would clearly be unacceptable to the Palestinians. The demand for recognition as a "Jewish" state was relatively new, added by the right-wing in Israel in recent years primarily in connection with the refugee issue in order to maintain a Jewish majority and thereby preserve the Jewish nature of the country. It was also problematic in part because of what it might mean for the Palestinian minority citizens of Israel, and in part because in Palestinian eyes this looked like racial (or religious) discrimination. There were Palestinians (and others) who went even further, arguing that a state could not be based on a religion (claiming that the Jews were co-religionists, not a people) and that recognizing Israel's right to exist did not mean according legitimacy to Zionism, namely the right of Jews to a state.

Israel also rejected the inclusion of the Arab League Resolution and Resolution 1397 as bases for a settlement, and it was not even willing to have Resolution 242 referred to except as an "outline" for future negotiations. The main reasons for these objections were not only the reference in the Saudi initiative to Resolution 194 but also the common point to them all: the need for Israel to withdraw to the 4 June 1967 lines—a line no government in Israel had been willing to accept officially since the 1967 war. Israel's interpretation of 242 had always been that it did not necessarily refer to all the territories occupied in 1967, and in time various Israeli leaders, including Rabin, had maintained that the West Bank technically was not included in Resolution 242 since it had not been under the sovereignty of any state when taken (Jordan's annexation of the West Bank after the 1948 war had been recognized by only two states) and was therefore "disputed territory." Israel also added a number of restrictions on the provisional Palestinian state, and as should have been expected, demanded that monitoring deal primarily with Palestinian compliance (and be under American management). It rejected any mention of the Bertini Report; it also rejected the inclusion of Syria and Lebanon in the plan as extraneous to the conflict with the Palestinians. The bulk of the remaining objections related to conditionality, greatly limiting any Israeli measures until and unless there were full Palestinian compliance with their obligations, some of which Israel embellished with even greater detail than the Quartet's document.

The Palestinian Authority also officially accepted the Road Map, but without submitting reservations. Indeed, wary of Israel's reservations, the Palestinians insisted that the Road Map not be altered or negotiated. They did, however, have concerns, particularly over the conditionality of the plan. They feared it might never get beyond its initial stages, and most problematically, it would never get out of the transition stage, Phase II. The idea of a state with provisional borders looked far too much like the long-term interim agreement Sharon had talked about in the past, which would be a territorial arrangement determined by Israel in accord with its interests and the status quo at the time, theoretically only temporarily but very likely to continue indefinitely. The fact that in its reservations Israel added certain demands for military and other restrictions on the Palestinian state with provisional borders, namely the state during the transition period, was indeed evidence that Israel viewed this as a period of significant duration (and not that envisaged by the Road Map's timeline, which Israel had said should only serve a reference point). In time the Palestinians were to suggest that Phase II be skipped all together, arguing that the Road Map presented this phase as an option only rather than a requirement.

The most important element of the Road Map from the point of view of the Israeli public was the first phase, in which there was to be an end to Palestinian violence and the beginning of security cooperation. Presumably of equal importance for the Palestinians was the requirement that Israel also abandon its use of force, such as house demolitions, curfews, and deportations. Neither side believed the document to be strict enough regarding these measures. Nonetheless, there was very high support among the Israeli public for the Road Map (sixty-five percent)[11] when it was presented, despite a very high degree of skepticism on both sides as to whether it would ever be implemented. Neither side thought the other would do what it was supposed to do, and given the ambiguous conditionality, especially as interpreted by Israel, it seemed unlikely that the Road Map would even get started. One could perhaps cynically argue that an "on-ramp" was needed to proceed onto the Road Map. In any case, the Road Map was pushed to the sidelines, at least temporarily, first by the Iraq War and then by Sharon's announcement of his Disengagement Initiative December 2003, in part in response to the Geneva Accord unveiled in October 2003.

CHAPTER TEN

The Geneva Accord—October 2003

Yossi Beilin, Justice Minister in Barak's government, a longtime leader of the peace camp, and one of the major negotiators at Taba, was convinced that sufficient progress had been made at Taba to enable the achievement of a final Palestinian-Israeli accord within a relatively short period of time. Whether or not this was the case was of no apparent interest to Sharon, for his responses to all the proposals since Camp David (and before) had been to postpone the possibility of final status negotiations, primarily by means of setting stiff preconditions. Moreover, the violent atmosphere of the Intifada and Israeli military actions, coupled with the post-Clinton policies of the United States (war on terror, war in Iraq), provided little potential for some kind of natural progression to peace talks even by means of the various proposals and plans such as the Road Map. Therefore, as he had in fact done upon occasion in the past, Beilin undertook his own informal negotiation. Together with Yasser Abd Rabbo, then Minister of Information in the PA, he created a group of Palestinians and Israelis that ultimately consisted of a number of leading security figures (including a former IDF chief of staff and a former head of Palestinian Preventive Security in the West Bank), as well as political, cultural, academic, and business figures, many of whom had participated in earlier formal negotiations.[1] After two years' work, on 12 October 2003 this team produced the Geneva Accord,[2] a detailed and comprehensive model for a final Israeli-Palestinian Peace Agreement to be signed by the State of Israel and the PLO.

The Accord addressed virtually every issue involved in the conflict, producing maps and devising mechanisms for implementation, in an effort to confront and resolve all the obstacles, pitfalls and lacunae of previous negotiations and proposals. In fact, the final version, as stated by the authors, closely followed the Clinton Parameters as a basis, in some instances incorporating the actual solutions proposed by Clinton. Most importantly, the Accord represented a combination of measures agreed to by a relatively varied and responsible group of Palestinians and Israelis who hassled over every word and debated over every line in an effort to produce a settlement that could be accepted by the majority of their peoples—not just by themselves.

In what had become standard form, the preamble of the Accord referred as a framework to all the UN resolutions since 1967, including 1397, and to all previous agreements and negotiations, including the Arab League Resolution, and also Bush's Rose Garden speech. Unlike other proposals, it added all of the Oslo agreements as well as Camp David, Clinton, Taba and the most recent, the Road Map. Also unlike all the previous proposals or plans, in the Geneva Accord the name "Palestine" was finally affixed to term "Palestinian state," replacing the PLO and the Palestinian Authority. Thus, the language of the Accord was to have psychological impact as well—for Palestinians to become accustomed to the State of Palestine as only part of historic Palestine, just as Israelis (and Jews everywhere) had become accustomed to the State of Israel as only part of the historic Eretz Israel (Land of Israel).

One of the most significant statements in the entire Accord was probably the preamble's affirmation that the agreement marked the "recognition of the right of the Jewish people to statehood," along with the same right of the Palestinians. To overcome the Palestinians' customary opposition to such a formula primarily because of the issue of the Israeli Arab minority, it went on to say "without prejudice to the equal rights of the Parties' respective citizens." But the formulation did squarely face the issue of the Jews, as a people, having a right to a state (the basis of political Zionism) just as the Palestinians, as a people, had a right to statehood. This position was strengthened by a statement in the body of the document recognizing "Palestine and Israel as the homelands [note: plural] of their respective peoples." Such affirmations, from a group of Palestinians that included important Fatah people as well as members of the PA administration, went a long way toward complying with Sharon's more recent conditions, as well as allying Israelis' fears.

▣ Outside Actors

Mechanisms for implementation (monitoring and verification), so sorely missing from all past proposals or as in the case of the Road Map inadequately accounted for, were provided in various forms. Actually there were probably too many such mechanisms, but this overcompensation was understandable in view of the fact that implementation had been a central problem with the Oslo Accords. In addition to a "ministerial-level Palestinian-Israeli High Steering Committee" that was to monitor as well as guide and facilitate implementation, there was to be an international Implementation and Verification Group (IVG), based in Jerusalem and consisting of representatives of the Quartet plus other countries agreed upon by the parties. Under the IVG there would be a Multinational Force (MF). The IVG itself would be headed by Contact Group (composed of senior political level representatives of all the groups in the IVG) who, in consultation with the parties, would appoint a Special Representative as the executive of the IVG on the ground. The Special Representative would appoint the commander of the MF. Implementation would be reviewed on a monthly basis in a meeting of Trilateral Committee composed of the Special Representative and the Palestinian-Israeli High Steering Committee, although this group could be convened with forty-eight hours if requested by any of the three components. The functions of the IVG were spelled out in some detail, and appeared also with regard to various topics such as Israeli withdrawals, dispute resolution, and security matters, but the overall function was to facilitate, assist in, guarantee, monitor, and resolve disputes relating to implementation of the Geneva Accord.

The composition, size and structure of the MF were to be determined in an annex to the Accord. The force was to be stationed in Palestine, with observers monitoring all the borders. The overall function of the MF was to monitor and verify for the implementation of various measures in the Accord, along with providing protection for both parties, protecting the territorial security of Palestine, deterring outside threat to it, and assisting the Palestinians in training and anti-terrorism measures. There were many more specific tasks for the MF detailed throughout the Accord, as with the IVG, in connection with specific security issues (Israel's early warning stations, border control, protection of the holy sites, and so forth). Still more detail was to be provided by annexes added later. Overall, however, and certainly in comparison with previous proposals, the Accord dealt in a comprehensive way with the role and authority of the MF so as to provide, together with the IVG and numerous bilateral organs, a practical, effective and acceptable mechanism to ensure implementation.

Outside parties were to play somewhat different roles with regard to matters connected with Jerusalem and with the refugee issue, for which an "international group" and an "international commission," respectively, were to be created. Their functions will be examined below, but the most significant aspect of the "international group" was its inclusion of representatives of the Organization of the Islamic Conference, who were to participate in a Multinational Presence on the Temple Mount/Haram al-Sharif. In general, these international bodies were to monitor implementation, though the Commission on the refugee issue would have additional functions, as will be illustrated below. In both cases, the involvement of outside parties went beyond the need for monitoring. The religious significance of the Temple Mount/ Haram al-Sharif, particularly as viewed by the Muslim world over the years, had been an argument (at Camp David and before) in opposition to Israeli sovereignty over the compound. And so the Accord finally conceded this matter, bringing in the Muslim world from outside (as distinct from purely Palestinian or the past Jordanian claims to control). The international element for the refugee issue was somewhat different—designed to accommodate Israel's opposition to assuming sole blame and therefore sole responsibility for the problem and its solution. Moreover, since the solution was to involve many nations, an international body would be needed to manage, not just monitor, implementation.

▣ Borders-Territorial Issues

The Geneva Accord stipulated that the border between the two states would be based on the 4 June 1967 lines, with equal "modifications" [swaps] on a one to one basis. The percentage of territory to be annexed by Israel, in exchange for an equal amount of territory to be annexed to the Palestinian state, was not specified. However, a map was referenced showing what would amount to approximately 2.7% of the West Bank remaining with Israel and an equal amount of land mainly next to the Gaza Strip but also two areas near the Hebron Hills that would go to the Palestinians. A joint committee was to determine the technical demarcation of the border, and the physical demarcation would be completed no later than nine months from the time the Accord went into effect. Israel was to assume responsibility for relocating the settlers outside Palestine, leaving the fixed assets and infrastructure in place for the Palestinians. Israel's evacuation, including that of the settlers, was to be carried out in stages, according to a timetable to be added in an annex to the agreement. However, the withdrawals were to begin immediately even though, according to the earlier clause, the border might not be physically demarcated until as much as nine months from the time the Accord went into effect.

The stages of the withdrawals, both in duration and location, were to be delineated in an annex but factors that would determine them would include the need to create contiguity and "early implementation" of Palestinian economic development, although it was not entirely clear just what this meant. Further factors were to be the building and functioning of the borders, along with the deployment of the multinational force, and finally Israel's capacity to "relocate, house and absorb" the settlers. All of this was not to be left open-ended, however. The first stage was to be completed within nine months, the

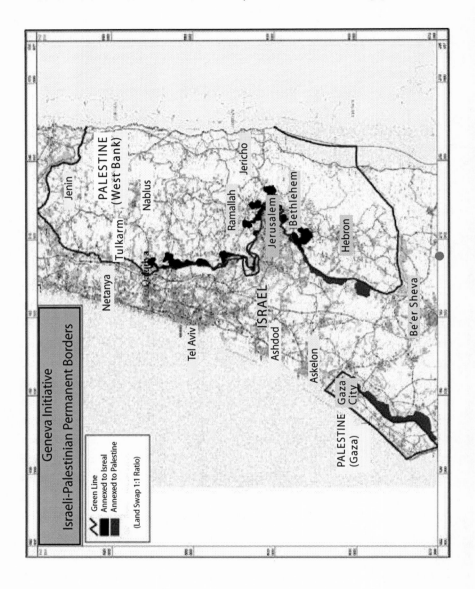

remaining areas to be fully evacuated no later than twenty-one months from the completion of the first stage. In other words, and explicitly stated, the total withdrawal was to be completed by no later than thirty months, six months less than that envisaged by Clinton, although Israel would keep a small military presence in the Jordan Valley for an additional three years. Surprisingly, it was not clear just when the State of Palestine was to be established. It may be assumed that it would exist once Israel completed its withdrawal, especially since the Palestinians were to move into and take control of every area as it was evacuated. Nonetheless, bearing in mind that the "provisional" state envisaged by Bush and the Road Map were not acceptable to the Palestinians, it is odd that the timing of the declaration of the state was not clearly stated, even if it was assumed that the state would be established as soon as the peace agreement were signed.

The long-delayed issue of safe passage for the Palestinians between the two parts of the Palestinian state was to be resolved by a corridor through Israel, connecting the Gaza Strip with the West Bank. Israel was to maintain sovereignty over the area of the corridor, meaning that it would not be counted as part of the Israeli territory Palestine was to receive in the swaps. However, the Palestinians would have responsibility for administration of the corridor, and persons using it would be subject to Palestinian law. The corridor would be fortified; and neither Palestinians nor Israelis would be permitted to enter the other's territory by means of the corridor. The issue of the roads in the West Bank was a bit more complicated, though extremely important because of the Palestinians' concern that Israeli interest in the use of certain roads was intended to cut Palestine into "cantons." The roads in question were three arteries in the West Bank which when used would permit more direct movement from one place in Israel (for example, Jerusalem) to another part of Israel (for example, Bet Shean in the northeast or Ein Gedi in the southeast, or simply from the center of the country to Jerusalem). Without using the word "sovereignty," Palestine was granted jurisdiction over these three roads, with the right to require permits for Israeli civilian use. The MF would patrol these roads at all times, without, however, prejudicing their use by the Palestinian security forces. As with the corridor through Israel, so too on these roads, Israelis would not be permitted to enter the State of Palestine.

▣ Security

Aside from the limited military presence in the Jordan Valley for possibly as long as five and a half years (down from the maximum ten years of Clinton and the twelve years proposed by Israel at Camp David), Israel was to have two early warning stations (down from the three of Clinton and the five Israel originally proposed at Camp David). Access to the early warning stations—which would mean military use of roads in the West Bank—would be guaranteed and escorted by the multinational force. Nothing was said in the Geneva Accord about access to the Jordan Valley by the small Israeli force, though it may be assumed that the same regulations would apply. Both the multinational force and the Palestinian security forces would maintain a presence in the early warning stations, thereby asserting Palestinian sovereignty but also ensuring some kind of control. The continued presence of the stations would be reviewed after ten years, and thereafter every five years, the implication being that this Israeli presence would be relatively prolonged—possibly even permanent. Similarly, the use of Palestinian airspace for Israeli Air Force training purposes was granted, but subject to review every ten years. Regulations for such usage were to be added in an annex to the Accord, but monitored for compliance by the International Verification Group. Thus on all three security issues (Israeli presence in the Jordan Valley, early warning stations, use of airspace) the Palestinians would be accommodating Israeli demands in principle, although Israel would compromise somewhat in execution (numbers, duration, MF and Palestinian roles, and so forth). Just the opposite was the case regarding border crossings. The Palestinian borders with Egypt and Jordan, plus the seaports and airports, would be manned by Palestinian security forces together with the MF. And Israel would maintain an unseen presence in both the passenger and cargo terminals at these entry points to Palestine. However, the multinational presence at the borders crossings was limited to five years, with subsequent annual approval by Palestine for any continuation. Similarly, the Israeli presence was limited to just thirty months, any subsequent Israeli control coming only from within Israel. The Palestinian security forces would be responsible for controlling the borders of Palestine, with the MF fulfilling the function of monitoring and verifying through the presence of its observers on the spot.

Palestine was to be a "non-militarized" state, thus the subtle Clinton semantics to indicate that the state would not be entirely "de-militarized" (though not the Palestinians' preferred "non-militarized") because Palestine would have a "strong security force." If the difference conceptually was not entirely clear from the semantics, the difference on the ground was quite clear by means of the clauses calling for limitations on the types of weapons the state would use, own, purchase for the security force or manufacture in the state. These limitations were probably to be similar to those of the Oslo Accords. They were to be added in an annex, subject to change only with the agreement of both parties and the MF or the IVG (like most other clauses in the Accord). No other individual or organization (besides the organs of the IVG, namely the MF) could "purchase, possess, carry or use weapons" except as provided by law. In another clause, it was stated that any "irregular forces or armed bands" should be dissolved and prevented. Altogether, these were another way of saying that there should be only one Palestinian security force, without, however, stipulating all the conditions or demands Israel and the United States had sought to impose on the Palestinians in the past (or listed in the Mitchell recommendations, for example) in this connection.

There were nevertheless certain requirements regarding terrorism and incitement. While nothing was said about destroying infrastructure, for example, the Geneva Accord did call on both sides to take "comprehensive and continuous" action to prevent and preempt terrorism, and also prosecute perpetrators. This was not to be left to the parties alone; a Trilateral Security Committee composed of the two parties and the United States would be formed to ensure implementation. It is only in connection with terrorism that the United States, and not the IVG or the MF, was designated as the outside monitor joining the two parties to the conflict. Presumably this especially reflected Israeli sensitivity on the subject. With regard to incitement, the IVG was considered sufficient to monitor implementation. Laws for the prevention of incitement to "irredentism, racism, terrorism and violence" were to be passed by both states, maintaining the reciprocity on this issue demanded by the Palestinians in the Wye Memorandum.

For the Palestinian public, one of the most important topics was that of the prisoners. Therefore, the prisoner releases promised by Oslo but which were only partially implemented were now clearly outlined (once again), along with stipulations for the release of additional prisoners. Ultimately all Palestinians and Arabs detained in connection with the conflict were to be released. This was to be done in three stages, starting immediately, according to different categories; all would be released within eighteen months of the entry into effect of the Accord. Only exceptional cases would have to wait a full thirty months, until the conclusion of the Israeli withdrawal. Further details were to be provided in an annex, but the categories clearly spelled out all administrative detainees (thereby, hopefully, ending a shameful chapter in the Israeli system of justice), as well as all persons arrested in connection with the conflict before and since Oslo.

The Geneva Accord contained an unusual reference, not present in previous proposals, to "regional security." The two sides were to pursue the establishment of a regional security regime, in cooperation with the neighboring countries and the international community. Not much was said about the nature of such a treaty or system beyond the generalities of seeking a stable peace without weapons of mass destruction and with a renunciation of the use of force. Nonetheless subsequent sections of the Accord referred to such a security regime. For example, with regard to the early warning stations, it was said that this matter might come under reconsideration if a regional security regime were established; with regard to the use of Palestinian roads, it was said that in the advent of regional peace, the Palestinian civilians might use Israeli roads. The addition of this section may have been a way of softening some of the Israeli security demands, using the argument that various measures were necessary only so long as a stable regional peace—and one that included Israel—did not exist.

▪ Refugees

The most important point with regard to the refugee issue was the right of return. This right as such is not stated anywhere in the Geneva Accord. Instead there is very careful wording recognizing the fact that with regard to the rights of the Palestinian refugees, Resolution 194, along with 242 and the

Arab League Resolution (called the Arab Peace Initiative), represent the basis for resolving the problem. Somewhat more directly, the rest of the clause goes on to say that the measures outlined in this section of the Accord will "fulfill these rights." Many Israelis view this as clear recognition of the right of return; many Palestinians, however, reject the Geneva Accord because they believe it does not recognize the right of return. Thus the attempt by the architects of the Accord to find a compromise phrasing was unsuccessful. This may have been due to the fact that logically speaking there is really no problem with recognizing a right (rights exist whether one recognizes them or not), especially if the exercise of that right is to be delineated both in substance and time—which is what the Accord did in fact do. Israel's argument generally had been that once such a right was recognized it could never be denied so that implementation would remain open-ended. In the eyes of the architects of the Accord, there was nothing open-ended about the agreement; the Accord explicitly stated that the implementation of the measures it outlined with designated time limits would both fulfill the rights and end all claims on this subject.

Moreover, the possibility that Israel would be inundated with an unlimited number of returning refugees was also ruled out by the clauses dealing with the refugees' choice of place of permanent residence. The formula used here was the same as that proposed by Clinton and adopted by the negotiators at Taba. Namely, refugees might choose between 1) the host country where they were presently residing, 2) the State of Palestine; 3) the areas being added to the Palestinian state in the swaps (once these areas were transferred to Palestine); 4) a third country; or 5) to Israel. All refugees would have the right to choose the Palestinian state (in accord with the laws of that state—presumably something similar to Israel's Law of Return for Jews). The choice of the present host or third countries would be dependent upon the "sovereign discretion" of the country in question, with numbers to be determined by each country. This clause was repeated specifically for Israel as well, namely that Israel would have sovereign discretion in the matter, and it would decide on the total number of refugees it would take. To prompt Israel to in fact permit the entry of refugees (presumably beyond the family reunification that Barak and past governments had been willing to offer), the Geneva

Accord went on to say that Israel "will consider," "as a basis," the average number being taken in by the different third countries. For Israel merely to "consider" this average did not bind it even to this number. Thus Israel, like the other states, would be the determining agent regarding the refugees it would take in. This, by the way, was the sense of the Arab League Resolution, which spoke of an "agreed upon" solution; it was also the sense that Palestinian leaders had been telling Israeli peace activists for many years.

Once the refugees' choices were submitted (no later than two years from the time implementation began) to an International Commission created to deal with the issue, and once the total numbers each country was willing to take had also been submitted, the International Commission would determine each refugee's permanent place of residence. The permanent residency itself was to be realized no later than five years from the creation of the commission, and once this was accomplished the refugees would no longer have refugee status. UNRWA would be phased out over this five-year period and refugees who had not submitted their applications within the first two years would lose their refugee status. Host countries in which refugees decided to remain would be provided "prompt and extensive" development and rehabilitation programs.

Both refugees and present host countries would be accorded compensation, and the Accord went into some detail in outlining just how this was to be determined and executed. An International Fund would be created for this purpose, and Israel would be a contributor along with the international community. Israel's total contribution (which could be paid in installments) would be based on the aggregate value of properties lost by the refugees' displacement and would be determined in a complex procedure by a panel of experts appointed by the commission, with consultants proposed and agreed upon by both Israel and Palestine. The value of the fixed assets that remained in Palestine from the evacuated Israeli settlements would be deducted from the sum Israel was to contribute. Once this final sum was determined, no further financial claims could be made against Israel. However, Israel would also contribute, along with other countries, to a Refugeehood Fund, administered by the commission to assist communal development in the areas formerly under UNRWA.

The members of the International Commission would be the Quartet, UNRWA, the Arab host countries, Switzerland, Canada, Norway, Japan, the World Bank and others to whom the parties (Israel and Palestine) might turn. While the commission would have overall responsibility for implementation of the measures connected with the refugee issue, it would create a large number of committees, funds and other entities—all included in some detail in the Accord—to deal with specific matters.

The very last item in the long list of matters treated in connection with refugees was a clause on Reconciliation Programs. This was perhaps the topic treated with the least detail in this section of the Accord, and virtually the only one lacking an organizational framework or modalities for funding. In fact it was vague, referring only generally to "encouraging and promoting" exchanges, civil society activities, cross-community cultural programs and the like in order to create greater understanding and appreciation of the narratives of each side. To the credit of the architects of the Accord it must be said that the addition, even of this brief mention of reconciliation, was an innovation that was missing from all previous proposals. That it should be so sparsely treated and vague and limited to the section on refugees was regrettable.[3] It has been said[4] that had there been a significant number of women among the authors of the Accord, this topic might well have been given far more treatment as a crucial, though subjective, element for a sustainable peace.

▣ Jerusalem

The very first sentence regarding Jerusalem established the "historic, religious, spiritual and cultural" attachment of the three religions, Judaism, Christianity and Islam, to the city. This may not have been just for the sake of acknowledging the importance of the religious sites but also to establish once and for all Israeli, and perhaps also Muslim, claims to the city—in view of the fact that both sides in the past had questioned the claims, at least on religious grounds, of the other side. There had been the argument that Mecca was far more important than Jerusalem for the Muslims, and that only the Arab-Israeli conflict had elevated the Haram al-Sharif, and with it Jerusalem, to a place of great importance. Similarly, Arafat had questioned Israel's claim to an historic-religious Jewish bond to the city, arguing that Jews had not even come to pray on the Temple Mount.[5]

The Geneva Accord dealt with the problems of Jerusalem in a most detailed fashion, but oddly—though presumably intentionally—it did not specify in the text what parts of the city would be under Palestinian sovereignty. Only by studying the detailed maps attached to the Accord could one learn what areas would go to which state, with regard to both the controversial settlements and suburbs of Jerusalem, as well as the various quarters of the Old City. There was no general explanation or sweeping statement of principle such as Clinton's "Arab neighborhoods to Palestine, Jewish neighborhoods to Israel." The critical phrase in the text was that the each state would have its recognized capital in the areas of Jerusalem under its sovereignty.

Since Jerusalem as a whole sits geographically within the boundaries of both states, the borders of the city were to be treated in the same way as the borders of each state. It was not clear, however, if the measures regarding border crossings were also to apply within the city for movement between Palestinian and Israeli sovereign neighborhoods. The clause regarding the border crossings for Jerusalem called for consideration of the special needs of the city, such as tourism and movement of Jerusalemites, which could be meant for either internal or outer borders. Presumably, however, the reference was solely for entry and exit to Jerusalem as a whole, inasmuch as there was a later reference in one clause to "the seam line" in Jerusalem, a term generally employed by the Israeli government to designate an unofficial line between East and West Jerusalem that was not to be considered a border dividing the city. If this is indeed the correct interpretation, movement within the city, between different sovereignties, was to be unimpeded, with the exception of the Old City.

There was far more clarity with regard to access to the Old City, the site of the majority of the holy places. There were in fact quite detailed guidelines for entry to and exit from the Old City. However, there was no mention of which quarter would belong to which state—certainly something that had been an important issue in past negotiations. The Accord stipulated that the Old City would be viewed as "one whole" entity, but the idea that this area would nonetheless be divided between the two states was indicated by a number of measures. For example, although there was to be free movement *within* the Old City, the modalities for entry into this area referred to the control of each party over the entry into its part of the Old City. Each party would police its own sovereign area in the Old City. And in addition a "visible color scheme" would be introduced inside the Old City to indicate the "sovereign areas of each party." Only the appended map revealed exactly which areas these would be and the fact the Jewish Quarter and approximately half of the Armenian Quarter (plus David's Citadel which would have special status) would be under Israeli control, and the rest Palestinian.

Far more clearly, and perhaps most importantly, the central and particularly difficult issue of the Temple Mount/Haram al-Sharif (dealt with as one Compound) was explicitly resolved. The Palestinians were to have sovereignty over the Compound once Israel had completed its withdrawal from the occupied territories, and Israel was to maintain sovereignty over the [Western] Wailing Wall. This had been Clinton's solution as well.

Aside from these crucial points of sovereignty, a large number of topics regarding the functioning and rights with regard to the city, and especially the holy places, were elucidated. Jerusalem was to have two municipalities, with an overall coordinating committee composed of the two parties, plus sub-committees for virtually all of the daily affairs (services and infrastructure) of the city, such as transportation, environment, water, planning and zoning, and policing, along with a separate sub-committee responsible for the joint provision of relevant services and functions for the Old City.

The Old City was to be under special regulations, designed to preserve its unique character and cultural heritage. For this purpose, the International Verification Group and an international consulting committee were to work closely with the joint municipal committee on the Old City. A separate Old City Police Unit was to be formed by the IVG to work with the Palestinian and Israeli police forces. The only arms permitted in the area would be those of the police forces, unless otherwise authorized. For security and intelligence, the Americans, rather than the IVG or the MF or any other third party, were to work with the two parties. Apparently this was due to the sensitivity over potential security problems in the Old City, which was similar to Israeli sensitivity and therefore demand that we saw above for U.S. involvement regarding the prevention of terrorism altogether. Another unusual measure was to be a special arrangement for the movement and security of Jews from the Jaffa Gate to the Zion Gate—a path through the Armenian Quarter on the way to the Jewish Quarter and the Wailing Wall. Nonetheless, as already noted, movement within the Old City was to be unfettered, but exit from it would be treated as a border crossing into the respective state. Citizens of either state could not exit the Old City without proper authorization; tourists could only leave through the state from which they entered. All these measures were to be subject to review after a period of three years from the time of transfer of authority over the Old City to the respective states (which apparently would come with the completion of Israeli withdrawal from Palestine).

As with the Old City, so too with regard to the Temple Mount/Haram al-Sharif compound, the Accord allotted special attention including extensive and detailed measures. In a sense the international arrangements for the compound were a replica of the overall international arrangements, namely, an International Group (which would actually include the IVG, and the two parties, plus others such as representatives of the Islamic Conference) and, in turn, would create a Multinational Presence (as distinct from the Multinational Force) to provide security and conservation of the compound. The latter, reporting to the International Group, would apparently have monitoring as well as dispute resolution tasks. Lest the granting of Palestinian sovereignty over the compound be interpreted as conceding Jewish historic and religious attachment to the site, the Accord referred specifically to the "unique religious and cultural significance" of the site to the Jewish people. To prevent what Israel feared might be desecration or even destruction of Jewish remnants there, and the Palestinian fear that Jewish excavations might topple the mosques above, the Accord ruled that any digging, excavation or construction would have to receive approval by both parties (namely, one of the alternatives Clinton had suggested). Similarly, the Palestinians were to ensure that no hostile acts against Israelis or Israeli areas emanated from the compound—this reference presumably being to the area of the Western Wall plaza. Thus the only arms to be permitted on the compound would be those belonging to the Multinational Presence and the Palestinian police. There was to be free access to the compound, subject to the customs already in place, including a reference to those set by the Wakf. (This may have been an indication that the Wakf was to continue to play a role in the administration of the compound but that was by no means clear in the document.) Authority over the compound was to be transferred to Palestine once the Israeli withdrawal was completed.

With regard to religious sites outside the city of Jerusalem, it was determined that access to them would be available to citizens of one state who would visit their sites in the other state by means of private shuttles. The sites listed were Rachel's Tomb, the Tomb of the Patriarchs in Hebron and Nabi Samuel, all of which would be in Palestine. No similar sites that might be located in Israel were listed for the Palestinians. In any case, additional sites were to be listed in an annex. The shuttle access would be escorted and protected by the MF, with local tourist police, while the sites would be administered jointly, although each state would be responsible for the protection and preservation of the sites on their territory.

The Accord also had clear provisions for resolution of disputes and promised additional articles on the water, economic relations and the law. However, these missing sections, together with the numerous annexes mentioned, have yet to be produced. Indeed some of the annexes, such as those connected with the multinational force or the transfer of authority or the early warning stations, along with the water issues or legal issues, for example, would deal with matters or details that might be critical to the implementation of the agreement. An additional problem was the abundance of bodies to be created to monitor, implement or assist in the functioning of the various solutions and provisions. Parsimony was clearly not a factor in the minds of the architects of the Accord. But their thinking may well have been that it would be better to err on the side of too much monitoring than too little, in view of past experience. Certainly the extensive involvement of third parties from the international arena could be viewed as an antidote to the lack of trust and initiative on the two parties themselves. And the addition of the Americans, specifically and exclusively on a number of the measures deemed particularly sensitive by the Israelis (such as counter-terrorism), served a similar purpose.

One might criticize specific territorial arrangements, which included or excluded one town or one settlement or another from the areas each side was to receive. Human rights and reconciliation were seriously neglected in the Accord (which may not have occurred had there been a number of women in the group). There were also Israelis who were not pleased with any international presence, particularly in Jerusalem. And the complicated arrangements for Jerusalem surely promised the advent of enormous traffic jams at the entrances to the city.

If there was more substantial or serious criticism, then it was over the very measures that were in fact the greatest achievements of the Accord: recognition of the Jews as a people with a right to a state (and Israel as the Jewish homeland), plus the trade-off between the right of return, on the one hand, and sovereignty over the Temple Mount/Haram al-Sharif on the other hand. Aside from religiously observant circles, there were also secular Israelis who argued that Israel should not abandon sovereignty over a symbol such as the Temple Mount. This, however, was not necessarily a view shared by a majority of Israelis. Not only are the majority of Israelis not religiously observant, but actually, although Jerusalem as a city is important—and no one wants to see a wall cutting it in two as before 1967—sovereignty over the area would only be an issue if it were created as such by the political right. The right wing had done so over the years, especially after Camp David, presenting the Temple Mount as a symbol of the Jewish link to Jerusalem, and it was likely to do so again. But this link was acknowledged in the Accord. And so long as important Jewish sites (such as the excavations along the Western Wall) were in Israeli hands or protected, it is very likely that most Israelis would be willing to forsake this abstraction (sovereignty) over a symbol in exchange for an end to the conflict. Palestinian abandonment of the demand for the right of return of all the refugees would indeed mean the end of the conflict, as explicitly stated in the Accord (both in the clauses stating that implementation of the agreement would constitute the end of the conflict, and in the section on refugees that stated that implementation would fulfill all the requirements and bring an end to all claims). The Palestinians understood this well, and indeed this was the major criticism on the Palestinian side, although in that community as well there were those who understood that there could not be an end to the occupation, and a chance for peace, if they were to insist on an open-ended right of return. The Geneva Accord presented a pragmatic solution, which demanded that the Palestinians abandon the last of their historic demands, and the dreams of most of the refugees or their descendants. Of course even this would not satisfy Israelis who opposed the immigration into Israel of any of the refugees, but these opponents presumably could be persuaded that the entry of perhaps 40,000, even 100,000 would hardly be a problem, particularly in view of the fact that Israel would be relieved of responsibility for over 200,000 Palestinian residents of East Jerusalem, to say nothing of the 3 million under occupation. It may be said, to quote Ghassan Khatib, a Minister in the Palestinian Authority who was not in the Geneva group, ". . . there is no doubt that when the two official governments sit for final status negotiations, they will benefit greatly from the ideas embodied in the Geneva Accord. *All that is required is the closing of some holes and finalizing of some important contours before the accord and all it represents can be actualized*"[6][emphasis mine].

The Geneva Accord received a mixed response amongst both populations. Within Israel, and to a lesser extent in Palestine, many concentrated on the persons involved in the Geneva group rather than the content of the proposed peace plan. In Israel the argument was that only elected officials, and specifically the government itself, had the right to negotiate. Moreover, the identification of Beilin with the Geneva Accord gave it the image of a left-wing-peace camp proposal, and one identified with the failed Oslo Accords at that. On the Palestinian side there was concern that unofficial talks had given away bargaining chips, or cards, thus hampering future negotiations. Moreover, both leaders, Beilin and Abed Rabbo, despite their past impressive status and influence, were in positions of descending power by the time the Accord was presented.

Nonetheless, there was and remained widespread support for the contents of the Geneva Accord. Immediately with publication and prior to the campaign promoting the model agreement, some forty-three percent of Israelis were said to support it, along with a similar percentage of Palestinians.[7] Arafat sent a letter of support to the official launch of the Accord in Geneva in December 2003, and Palestinian Prime Minister Ahmed Qureia (Abu Ala) also expressed his personal support in a meeting with a delegation of Americans for Peace Now a month earlier. The Accords revived the peace camp in Israel, providing it not only with substance to advocate but also with proof that there were Palestinian partners for peace (indeed one of the objectives of the Geneva group). Ironically, by presenting a model for a final accord, it also served to bring out of obscurity and actually strengthen another final-status initiative, the far less ambitious Nusseibeh-Ayalon Petition. Still more importantly, the Geneva Accord sparked the only major project in the direction of peace to be undertaken by the Sharon government: the Disengagement Plan for withdrawal from Gaza.

CHAPTER ELEVEN

The Nusseibeh-Ayalon Petition (The Peoples' Voice)—July 2002

The Peoples' Voice, as it was called in English, had also been presented during the al-Aksa Intifada over a year before the Geneva Accord and was a less ambitious project. Although it also sought to provide a basis for a final peace accord, in itself certainly an ambitious goal, it did not seek to create a model for such an agreement. Rather, it presented a set of principles, just six in number. These addressed the central issues of the conflict, in particular those that had been the focus of attention in Camp David and Taba. One might find hints of the Clinton Parameters in this initiative as well, but it was almost totally lacking even in the details provided by Clinton. Indeed, the absence of detail was intended as the strength of the initiative. The idea was to present the bottom lines, so to speak, upon which the two sides could agree, leaving the details for official negotiations.

The intention was to sign a million (later termed simply "masses") of Israelis and Palestinians on these principles as an instrument of pressure on the two governments to resume negotiations. Thus unlike Geneva, the purpose was not to prove that there was a partner, although that might be a side-effect, but rather to create a ground-swell of public pressure not identified with the peace camp or political figures but composed of numbers, large ones. It was termed a civil initiative, in order to dissociate it from identification with any political party or camp—out of a certain disdain for party politics and a wish to appeal to a broad public beyond that of the peace camp.[1] Thus, whereas Geneva emphasized both the importance and influence of its group to demonstrate that peace could be made with central and powerful personalities on both sides, the Peoples' Voice emphasized just the opposite to demonstrate that the grassroots of their societies sought peace and wanted to be heard.

The initiator of the campaign was Ami Ayalon, former commander of the Israeli navy and former head of the General Security Services (Shin Bet), a highly respected and at the time an independent (not party affiliated) public figure. His Palestinian counterpart became Professor Sari Nusseibeh, President of Al Quds University in East Jerusalem, the scion of a prestigious Jerusalem family and an influential member of the Palestinian political elite, formerly the PLO official responsible for Jerusalem. Though a member of Fatah, Nusseibeh was known for his independence and original thinking.

The Petition laid out the agreed principles, the implementation of which would constitute the end of all claims on both sides and the end of the conflict. The first and basic principle was two states for two peoples. Both sides were to declare that Palestine was "the only state of the Palestinian people" and Israel "the only state of the Jewish people." Thus, the Jews were recognized as a people, with, by implication, a right to their own state. The term "only" was presumably employed not because Jews might claim another state (an idea that had never been heard) but because Nusseibeh had argued in the past that the right of return would result ultimately in a Palestinian majority in Israel, which would give the Palestinians two, not just one, state. Therefore, it needed to be clearly stated that the Palestinians did not intend to infringe on the Jews' statehood.

This position, designed to allay Israeli fears, was made still clearer in the principle regarding the refugees. Entitled the "Right of Return," this return was to be limited explicitly to the State of Palestine, with the additional provision that Jews were to return only to the State of Israel. The last may have been included simply to provide symmetry, but it was reminiscent of a slogan aimed at present or potential Jewish settlers: Jews give up their right of return to the Land of Israel, Palestinians give up their right of return to historic Palestine. The same clause acknowledged the suffering of the Palestinian refugees, without assigning responsibility. Israel, together with Palestine, would contribute to international funds that would provide compensation to the refugees and assistance for the welfare of those who decided to remain where they presently resided or those who moved to a third country.

In keeping with the idea of each people having just one state, and return being only to one's own state, the Petition stated that no settlers would remain in the state of Palestine once the final borders were established. These "agreed borders" were to be based on the 4 June 1967 lines, UN resolutions, and the Arab (Saudi) peace initiative. As in the Geneva Accord, the addition of the reference to 1967 and the Saudi initiative was to ensure that Israel's loose interpretation of Resolution 242 would not pertain. (The reference to what the Petition called the "Arab peace initiative" was inserted only in the section on borders, presumably lest its references to the refugee issue be implied.) The reference to 1967 was of course more explicit than Barak had been willing to be at Camp David, but the Petition was also more generous than he had been. The Petition called for border modifications based on swaps, in this case, equal one to one territorial exchanges in keeping with the needs of both sides, including security but also demographic considerations and territorial contiguity. It was not entirely clear if the reference to demography meant simply that communities should not be divided by the border or if it referred to a broader issue of reducing the number of Palestinians under Israeli control. It may have been an oblique reference to the size of territory Israel would annex in order to maintain settlements (namely, something like the eighty percent of the settlers that Barak had sought to accommodate in large settlement blocs). A connection was assured between the two parts of Palestine, the Gaza Strip and the West Bank.

The only thing said about security was that the Palestinian state would be demilitarized (not the non-militarized expression of Clinton), and the international community would "guarantee its security and independence." There was no explanation as to what was to be involved in a "guarantee." There was somewhat more elucidation on the issue of Jerusalem. Here part of the

Clinton proposal was adopted: Arab neighborhoods to be under Palestinian sovereignty; Jewish neighborhoods under Israeli sovereignty. Jerusalem was to be an open city, with free access for all to all the religious sites. A suggestion that had been raised by the Americans at Camp David was stipulated in order to resolve the Temple Mount/Haram al-Sharif sovereignty question. Neither side would have sovereignty. The Palestinians would be custodians ("guardians") of the Haram al-Sharif for the benefit of the Muslims. The Americans had advocated this earlier as an arrangement similar to that of Saudi Arabia with regard to Mecca and Medina. Israel would have guardianship of the Western Wall for the benefit of the Jewish people. It was added that no excavations could take place without mutual consent. The Christian sites, which in any case had not been the subject of any previous controversy between Israel and the Palestinians, would remain as they were.

The document was thus short and concise—though perhaps too concise. It probably had enough for the average Israel since it clearly ruled out the return of any refugees to Israel and did not explicitly give away the Temple Mount. However, this resolution of the Temple Mount/Haram al-Sharif problem still would not meet the objections of those who believed in the value of sovereignty over this symbol. Certainly both these proposals would find greater support among Israelis than either the Clinton Parameters or the Geneva Accord solutions. Similarly, a demilitarized Palestine would suit Israelis, although the absence of any stipulations regarding security arrangements could raise objections. The real problem, however, would lay with Palestinian acceptance. The Petition did build on a trade-off between the right of return and the Temple Mount/Haram al-Sharif, but it is hard to believe that many Palestinians would relinquish the idea of *any* refugees returning, at least as put in such definitive terms. The Geneva Accord too avoided the right of return, but it at least allowed for some refugees to seek entry to Israel, and it put the matter in somewhat more flexible terms without abandoning Israel's virtual veto power over numbers and the conclusion of the problem. The Geneva Accord also made the trade-off complete by according sovereignty over the Temple Mount/Haram al-Sharif to the Palestinians.

While meeting some of the Palestinian needs, particularly regarding the borders and the settlements, the Petition was a document more favorable to

Israel than the Palestinians. In addition, the Israeli initiator, Ami Ayalon, may have been an asset for promulgation of the Petition in Israel because of his legitimacy as a security figure, but in the eyes of Palestinians he was the former head of the hated Shin Bet and therefore a good reason to oppose the initiative. Nusseibeh for his part was very acceptable in Israeli eyes, having made innovative and moderate statements in the past, including the one about giving up the right of return because it implied two rather than one Palestinian state. Among Palestinians, however, he was a respected but controversial intellectual with only a limited following.

Be that as it may, by late summer 2005, the organizers claimed to have signed some 161,000 Palestinians to the document, along with 254,257 Israelis.[2] The publication of the Geneva Accord had actually helped the Petition among Israelis, by demonstrating that there was a partner. And a concise set of principles, blunt and unambiguous on the refugee issue, appeared to carry greater appeal than a detailed plan like the Geneva Accord. The relatively large number of Palestinian signatures may attest more to the respect for Nusseibeh than actual agreement with the content of the Petition, but if 161,000 Palestinians were willing to affix their names to the petition's principles, it seemed to bode well for future attempts at reaching peace.

CHAPTER TWELVE

The Disengagement Plan— 2003–2005

At the Herzliya Conference of the private Israeli university The Interdisciplinary Center, Herzliya, on 18 December 2003, Sharon revealed his initiative for a unilateral withdrawal from some territory and settlements. Later these were revealed to be the Gaza Strip and four isolated, nearly empty settlements in the northern part of the West Bank.[1] The political strategy behind the initiative—called the Disengagement Plan— remained unclear, if indeed Sharon had a clear strategy in mind at the time or later. In the past, Sharon had spoken of a long-term interim agreement by which Israel would hold onto most of the territories (around two-thirds) and the Palestinians would have control over various areas (possibly conceived as "Bantustans"). He may have perceived the disengagement as a unilateral version of this idea, possibly intending the separation barrier already under construction on the West Bank as an added component.[2] Thus, strategically the idea may have been to jettison the Gaza Strip, with all its human as well as security problems, while solidifying Israel's hold over the majority of the West Bank. The tactical reasons for the disengagement idea, however, were a bit clearer than the strategic considerations.

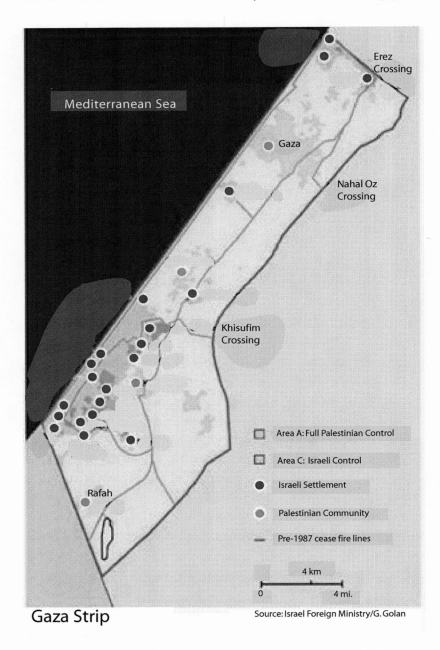

Mediterranean Sea

Erez
Crossing

Gaza

Nahal Oz
Crossing

Khisufim
Crossing

Area A: Full Palestinian Control

Area C: Israeli Control

Israeli Settlement

Palestinian Community

Pre-1987 cease fire lines

4 km

0   4 mi.

Rafah

Gaza Strip

Source: Israel Foreign Ministry/G. Golan

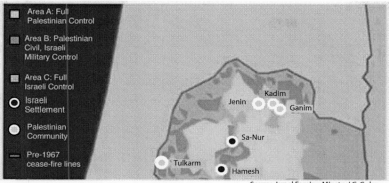

Area A: Full Palestinian Control

Area B: Palestinian Civil, Israeli Military Control

Area C: Full Israeli Control

○ Israeli Settlement

● Palestinian Community

— Pre-1967 cease-fire lines

Northern West Bank

Source: Israel Foreign Minstry/ G. Golan

In the months preceding Sharon's announcement of his Disengagement Plan, there had been increasing signs of dissatisfaction and protest within the Israeli public. A relative calm in the violence, namely a reduction in the terrorist attacks, which was brought to a sudden halt by an exchange of violence (Israeli targeted killing/Palestinian terrorist attack/Israeli show of force) may have served as a backdrop to intensified expression of opposition to the status quo and demands to open a political path. A chain of events may have disturbed Sharon himself: a letter signed by IDF pilots (the elite of the IDF) refusing to serve or support the present policies; apparently critical comments made even by the Chief of Staff; protests by soldiers protecting settlements in Gaza; and perhaps most importantly, criticism of the government expressed by four former heads of Israel's security services in an extensive interview in the Israeli press. Into this accelerating chain of protest came the announcement of the Geneva Accord, offering a concrete, even detailed, policy alternative. This chain of events catapulted the annual Rabin memorial rally of early November 2003 into a massive protest demonstration organized by the Israeli peace camp. One month later, Sharon launched his initiative.

A contributing factor may well have been extensive comments in the press and elsewhere that finally drove home to the right wing the changing demographics of the area. It may be that it had finally become clear to Sharon that very shortly Jews would be a minority in the area between the Jordan River and the Mediterranean Sea. Such a situation would lead either to an apartheid situation—an Israeli minority denying basic rights to an Arab majority population under its control, or the extension of rights to all, leading ultimately to a bi-national state, which would in fact be the end of the Zionist ideal of a state for the Jewish people; the Jews would become a minority population in their historic homeland as in the Diaspora. It may be in response to this realization that Sharon decided it was time to act unilaterally to reduce the Arab population under Israeli control by 1.3 million (the population of the Gaza Strip) and thereby at least postpone the demographic sword of Damocles. At least official voices from Sharon's supporters and occasionally from Sharon himself could be heard referring to the demographic logic behind the Disengagement, alongside the comment that Israel needed to come up with some initiative lest an unpalatable plan be forced upon it (meaning the Geneva Accord or perhaps the Road Map), presumably by the international community or even the Americans.

The Disengagement Plan itself, as officially presented on 28 May 2004, would not necessarily have ended the occupation of Gaza, despite its stated claim to do so and the potential it had for doing so.[3] What the status of the area of the settlements to be evacuated in the northern West Bank would be was also unclear. In the Gaza Strip, as presented, Israel would not only withdraw all military and settler personnel, it would relinquish all governmental authority within the Gaza Strip, as it did under the Oslo Accords in area A, thereby technically ending its occupation, at least as Israel saw it. Yet Israel was to maintain control of all access to the Strip, by sea, air and land, including the stationing of troops in what was called the Philadelphi corridor between Gaza and Egypt. Further, Israel reserved the right to "preventive measures as well as the use of force against threats originating in the Gaza Strip." To this was added Israel's control over infrastructure (for example, the supply of electricity and clean water[4]), vital to the Palestinians. Further, all arrangements, whether for future relations, entry and exit of goods or persons, as well as for the withdrawal itself, the disposition of assets and lands, or similar issues, was to be determined unilaterally by Israel. Sharon repeated often that there would be no negotiation with the Palestinians regarding the Disengagement.

All of these limitations could have made (and perhaps were intended by Sharon to make) the plan more palatable to the hawks within his government and party. A more cynical interpretation might be that unilateral withdrawal under these circumstances and conditions would leave chaos in its path, resulting in internal violence and instability—thereby offering a useful example of the pitfalls and undesirability or efficacy of further withdrawals—for example, from the West Bank.

Not all the problems or flaws in the plan were necessarily purely fabricated or politically motivated. There was a very real and legitimate Israeli concern over the possibility of post-withdrawal smuggling of weapons into the Gaza Strip and continued terrorist attacks from the area. There were genuine concerns about political and security instability after withdrawal, concerns shared by the Palestinians as well. Further, perhaps most importantly, there were serious Palestinian economic concerns: the ability of Gaza to survive without the Israeli infrastructure should this be abandoned, as well as without control over import and export activity, free movement of personnel and goods—particularly with the West Bank, and the division or dispensation of assets left behind or destroyed once joint ventures such as the industrial parks were disbanded. Israel was also planning to remove Gaza from the jurisdiction of the Paris economic accords, including its allowance for a customs union. Moreover, economic collapse would have ramifications for Israeli security as well. A list of problems would therefore include: 1) the borders (what was called the "envelope" of sea, air and land access); 2) internal security; 3) dispensation of property and economic assets left behind; and 4) economic rehabilitation. Additionally, there were more political questions such as 5) the relationship and connection of Gaza to the Palestine Authority in the West Bank; 6) the legal status of Gaza ("sovereign," "unoccupied," "self-ruling entity");[5] and 7) the political future—was this to be a first step toward the end of the occupation altogether, or merely a one-time affair? And how could all these problems be resolved if Israel insisted upon acting totally unilaterally?

Several things interceded, leading to a change in some of the elements and problems of the Disengagement Plan. First was the strong American support for the Plan, seen by Washington as part of, rather than a substitute for, the Road Map and a step along the path to peace. Indeed the Americans increasingly characterized the withdrawal (a term avoided by Sharon and his government) as a courageous concession by Sharon. The second important interceding factor was the death of Arafat, whose obstinacy, according to Sharon, was the major reason that Israel had to act unilaterally. The election of the moderate Abu Mazen, his swift achievement of a ceasefire among the Palestinian factions, and his clearly enunciated policy in favor of a peaceful solution of the conflict significantly altered the context in which the Plan was to be implemented. This is not to say that that the matter of post-disengagement security both within and from Gaza was now resolved. Abu Mazen was indeed locked in a fateful struggle with the Islamists (Hamas and the Islamic Jihad) and even radical elements of his own Fatah party over both power and policy. But a decided change in atmosphere and prospects did create pressure upon Sharon to move closer to a genuine end of the occupation of Gaza and engage in some coordination with the Palestinian leadership, though not actual negotiations. In fact it was probably wise not to open negotiations as such over the Disengagement Plan, for that would have perhaps delayed implementation indefinitely as quid pro quo measures were debated. However, coordination was important in order to ensure the smooth execution of the withdrawal and some stability for the future by jointly resolving some of the problems and thereby strengthening Abu Mazen politically.

The result was a somewhat modified plan involving the important introduction of a third party. Most significantly perhaps, Sharon abandoned the idea of maintaining an Israeli military presence in the Philadelphi corridor. Instead, Egyptian military forces would be deployed along this part of Gaza-Egyptian border instead of the small police force Egypt had been limited to in that area according to the Israeli-Egyptian Peace Agreement of 1979. Thus Israel would entrust to its former enemy, Egypt, the prevention of arms smuggling and terrorist infiltrations into the Gaza Strip, a move that marked the extraordinary amount of trust that had developed between the two countries over the intervening years. The Egyptian role went a long way toward paving the way for genuine Israeli military withdrawal from the Gaza Strip. The question over one of the crossing points (Rafah) on the Egyptian border still remained. Israel wanted to continue to control it, but in the end a European presence on the Palestinian side was agreed upon instead.

The Egyptians also undertook to train and assist the formation of an effective Palestinian security force in Gaza, including training on the spot as well as in Egypt. Further third-party involvement was undertaken by the G-8 and the World Bank as well as the Quartet's special envoy for the development of Gaza, James Wolfensohn.[6] Wolfensohn, along with World Bank officials, became involved not only in economic planning and development matters, including the problem of maintaining the economic link between Gaza with the West Bank, but also assisted in the resolution of many of the practical problems connected with the evacuation and transfer of power from Israel to the PA. The British and other EU experts were sent to assist in security matters and the Americans sent General William Ward initially for six months (succeeded by General Keith Dayton) to guide the Palestinian security reforms. Sharon agreed in principle to the building of the seaport with, apparently, European supervision to replace that of Israel (although Israel would maintain its control of the territorial waters off the coast of Gaza); and Sharon was apparently considering the reopening of the airport, possibly also to have European supervision.[7] Finally, in the last months prior to the Disengagement itself, coordination with Abu Mazen's government was finally initiated, with the help of the Egyptians and Wolfensohn, leading to agreements on the disposition of physical assets and other issues.[8]

From its initial presentation, the Disengagement Plan met with decisive and vociferous opposition not only from the settler movement but also from Sharon's own party. Misjudging the situation, Sharon agreed to a poll within his party only to have the majority vote against the Plan. Sharon proceeded in any case, dismissing right-wing members of his government and ultimately reshuffling his government to bring in the Labor Party in order to gain majority support within the cabinet while relying on the opposition party, Meretz, for a majority in the Knesset. The majority of the Israeli public at large supported the Plan, with surveys wavering around the sixty percent (sometimes higher, sometimes lower), although there was much skepticism as to whether Sharon would actually go through with the Plan. To a large degree, skepticism was based on the numerous political hurdles and the long period—one and a half years—that was to intervene before implementation was to take place in the summer of 2005. Most importantly, however, the settler movement, closely tied to and represented by the once moderate National Religious Party and fortified by the extreme right-wing parties, launched an all-out and sometimes violent campaign against the Disengagement Plan.

Sharon may have been surprised by the negative reception not only from the settlers but also from within his party, particularly in view of the limited nature of the Plan initially. The evacuation of a little more than two dozen settlements (some with no more than a few families) and relocation of no more than 7,500 residents (according to some counts 1,500 families) would hardly make a dent in the 240,000 plus number of settlers in all the occupied territories. Nor would it be a difficult matter, in terms of logistics, for a country like Israel that had handled massive immigrations in the tens and hundreds of thousands of persons over short periods of time. Nor would the dismantling of a limited number of settlements in the Gaza Strip and four small isolated ones in the northern part of the West Bank necessarily have constituted a precedent for an irreversible process. Jewish settlements in the Sinai had been dismantled in the context of the peace accords with Egypt, even at the initiative of the man greatly responsible for putting them there, Ariel Sharon.[9]

The settler leadership itself, however, decided to make this move a critical battle. It was not the value of these particular settlements or even of the territory (the Gaza Strip) involved, but in the eyes of the settler leadership and much of the settler community and their supporters, it was the principle of this withdrawal that would determine the future of Israel's control over all the territories conquered in 1967. Regardless of whatever had been done over twenty years ago with the Sinai settlements, and regardless of future intentions, the settler movement made the Disengagement the supreme test— could Israel in fact leave the territories? With a scare campaign that included threats of resistance even to the point of violence and civil war, along with a well-organized, well-financed emotional campaign amongst the Israeli public against "uprooting" or "transfer" of Jews from homes in which many had been living for over a generation, a move described as "a reward for terrorism," the settler movement hoped to corrode popular support for Disengagement. Initially they believed these tactics, along with refusal to cooperate with the government's relocation and compensation plans, would lead to cancellation of the Plan. Thus, as the argument went, if a government under a strong right-wing leader like Ariel Sharon proved unable to do it, clearly no one in the foreseeable future could hope to dislodge the settlers, not from a relatively unimportant and unpopular place like the Gaza Strip and certainly not from ideologically and religiously more important places like the West Bank and East Jerusalem. Moreover, if the evacuation were in fact to take place but in the form of a national trauma, possibly even civil war, no political party would be willing to undertake such a problematic endeavor again in the future.

Indeed the settlement project as envisaged and undertaken under Sharon in the late 1970s (as distinct from the relatively small settlement ventures under Labor governments) had been intended to bring about this very impossibility, namely, withdrawal from the territories. Sharon's announced goal in 1979 of settling 100,000 Jews in the occupied territories was designed both to prevent any pulling apart of the area, so to speak, that is, territorial compromise, and to prevent the creation of a Palestinian state. The policy of offering lucrative economic incentives for Jewish settlement was then instituted to overcome the limited number of ideological settlers—those who would go there for nationalist/religious reasons. The idea was to create a constituency that would, for practical reasons, be opposed to withdrawal. And the policy did in fact lead to over 240,000 settlers, some seventy percent of whom were to describe their reason for going there as an interest in "quality of life" (a euphemism for economic reasons) as distinct from national or religious reasons.[10] Thus the settlements were meant as an obstacle to compromise— and by implication to peace. If the day were to come, this would be the test: could this body of people be dislodged, could the settlements be evacuated so that Israel could withdraw? Such was the issue the settler movement placed before the public and the government in its response to the Disengagement Plan.

That is why implementation of Sharon's disengagement initiative became crucial to the peace process. This head-on collision with the settler movement need not have come at this time, specifically around this Plan, but that is what the settler movement turned it into: a day of reckoning over the territories that Israeli society, divided since 1967 into doves and hawks and just plain confused, had known would come eventually. The potential outcome was not

Israeli Settlements and Outposts—2006

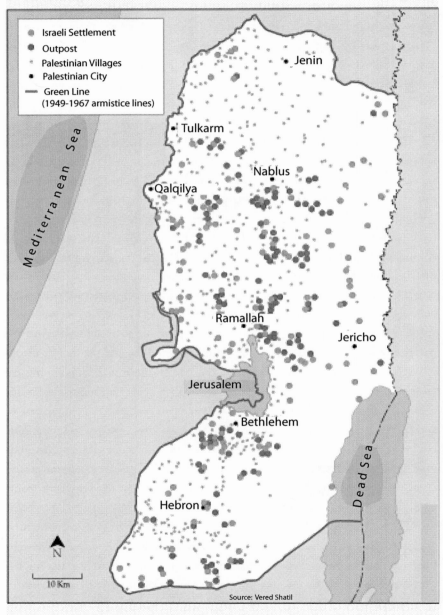

entirely clear. For many years, public opinion in Israel had been relatively consistent in its agreement to territorial compromise, the evacuation of most or all of the settlements, and a two-state solution with the Palestinians. And if these were the alternatives offered now, namely a peace agreement, the evacuation of the Sinai settlements over twenty years ago would and could have served as an appropriate precedent. But Sharon's Plan offered no such incentive; it did not come in the context of a peace agreement or even the promise of one. And therefore the settlers' arguments met with little to no response from the government. The majority of the public favored disengagement from Gaza because it considered the area a hell-hole, believed the settlements there to serve no purpose, and saw no reason for endangering soldiers' lives to protect them. But the official response could not use these arguments without admitting its own responsibility for putting the soldiers and settlements there in the first place. Instead its feeble, sometimes only indirect references to the real reasons for the Plan, were unconvincing, blurring, perhaps intentionally, the real but unintended, significance of the plan: the test of Israel's ability to take down settlements—a *sine qua non* for any future agreement for the end of occupation and end to the conflict.

The Disengagement Plan was implemented; the evacuation of the settlements took place and far more swiftly than anticipated, albeit with some minor violence on the part of fanatic elements, many if not most of whom were not even residents of the settlements targeted by the Plan. Many of the scenes were indeed dramatic and even traumatic for viewers as well as participants, and there was sympathy for people having to leave their homes unwillingly. On balance, however, the settler movement overplayed its hand. The challenge to the government and army, the near rebellion against democratically determined and judicially endorsed decisions of the Knesset, the incitement, obstructive tactics, insensitive slogans and gimmicks, particularly the use of Holocaust symbols and analogies, all alienated much of the public. In the final analysis, the settlers lost. It was proven that withdrawal, including evacuation of settlements, was possible. Whether this would continue in a unilateral form or by means of an agreement was yet to be determined, but the successful dismantling of the settler enterprise in at least Gaza and part of the West Bank could be expected to have important repercussions with regard to the possibilities for peace and the peace plans still being formulated. Even as the process was taking place, the United States made it clear that it viewed this disengagement as but one concession Israel must make and as part of a revived Road Map.

CHAPTER THIRTEEN

U.S.-Israel Understandings: Bush and Weissglas Letters

With the advent of the Disengagement Plan, two sets of letters between the United States and Israel asserted certain understandings between the two governments on controversial issues. Sharon had presented a draft of his Disengagement Plan to the American president even before making it public in Israel or submitting it for approval to his own cabinet. In his 14 April 2004 letter accompanying the proposed Plan, Sharon explained the unilateral nature of the Plan (using the terms "villages and towns" for the settlements to be evacuated), repeated Israel's demands regarding the Palestinians, and agreed to certain Israeli steps, namely limitations on the growth of settlements and dismantling of the "unauthorized outposts."[1] Nonetheless he explained that Israel would accelerate the construction of the "security fence." Though not stated explicitly in Sharon's letter, he offered the Disengagement Plan as a significant Israeli concession, for which he sought certain commitments from the United States in exchange. These commitments were of great importance, and they would also be useful for Sharon in his subsequent effort to get the Disengagement Plan accepted by his government and party.

Bush obliged with the introduction of two significant changes in what had been standard American policies regarding both the refugee issue and the settlements, along with a slight change in the newer policy regarding the separation barrier. Regarding the refugee issue, in his letter of 14 April, Bush did not make do with the general formulations of the Road Map or past declarations.[2] He met Israel's demand directly in stating that the refugee problem was to be solved within the Palestinian state "rather than Israel," affirming American support for Israel as a Jewish state. This, of course, meant that the United States was placing its stamp of approval on Israel's position, but it also meant that what might have been a negotiating position, to be exchanged for an Israeli concession in negotiations, was lost for the Palestinians—i.e., the final position on the refugee question would, at least in US and Israeli eyes, now be a foregone conclusion.

The second American commitment was abandonment of Washington's official position in opposition to the building of settlements in the occupied territories—an opposition that had been based on the Fourth Geneva Convention, which explicitly banned settlement in occupied territory. Responding to Sharon's requests, albeit in keeping with many of the plans that had been proposed in past negotiations including Camp David, Taba and the Clinton Parameters, the United States implicitly supported the maintenance of Israeli settlement blocs as part of a final status agreement. The language of the letter was less explicit. Bush explained that it would be "unrealistic" to expect a return to the 4 June 1967 lines (he said the 1949 armistice lines, an accurate but subtly more justifiable description of the pre-'67 border). The reason was the "new realities on the ground, including already existing population centers." One might interpret this along the lines of America's traditional position in favor of the 1967 lines with minor adjustments, but the reference to population centers and realities on the ground strongly suggested much more than minor border changes. Indeed this is how Israel and the rest of the world, including the Palestinians, interpreted it, and this is how Sharon presented it to the Israeli public—in exchange for giving up a few settlements in Gaza. Inasmuch as Bush did not add any specifics, such as naming Ariel—a large West Bank settlement that was the subject of controversy between Washington and Sharon in the context of the separation barrier—he did leave room for other interpretations in the future. And some consolation might be derived from the fact that Bush ignored Sharon's characterization of the Gaza settlements as "villages and towns." Nonetheless, Bush's letter represented a new American position.

Further, the Bush letter provided at least partial—although only partial—support for the building of the separation barrier, despite the fact that the International Court of Justice in the Hague was in the process of issuing an opinion on its legality due to its construction partially within the West Bank itself. The president's letter acknowledged and repeated the assurances Sharon had included in his letter regarding the separation barrier. These assurances were that the "barrier ...should be a security rather than a political barrier, should be temporary rather than permanent," and therefore would not prejudice the final status agreement on borders. Moreover, the president added, as a gentle limitation on Israel, that the route of the barrier should take into account, subject to Israel's security needs, the "impact on Palestinians not engaged in terrorist activities." Although American reservations regarding the separation barrier apparently remained, there was nothing in this text to prevent Sharon from continuing construction as planned. In fact the only concrete limitation placed on the demarcation of the barrier was that handed down by the High Court of Israel some months later.

On 19 April 2004, a few days after this exchange of letters at the highest level, there was a letter to then National Security Advisor Condoleezza Rice from Sharon's bureau chief Dov Weissglas specifying the commitments Israel made to the US in exchange for the Bush commitments.[3] In addition to repeating word for word President Bush's language regarding the separation barrier, Israel promised to work with the Americans to define the boundaries of permitted construction within the existing settlements and to provide a list of outposts to be dismantled, with dates. This information was to guide Israel in its promise to refrain from settlement expansion and to dismantle the outposts. Neither of these two commitments was met. However, the fact that the United States continued to demand construction limitations for the settlements and dismantling of outposts suggested that America's revised position on the settlements expressed in Bush's letter did not mean blanket approval for settlement expansion.

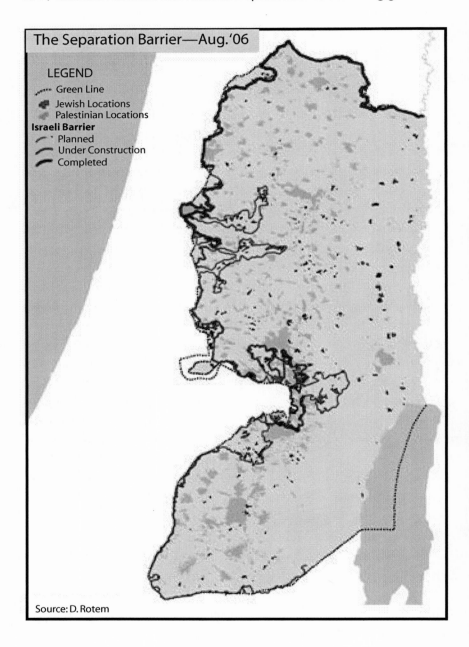

The Separation Barrier—Aug. '06

LEGEND
Green Line
Jewish Locations
Palestinian Locations
Israeli Barrier
Planned
Under Construction
Completed

Source: D. Rotem

According to the Weissglas letter, similar commitments were made regarding the lifting of roadblocks and checkpoints, subject to security considerations, along with a commitment regarding the transfer of Palestinian revenues to the PA pending Israeli court decisions. Weissglas reiterated Israel's commitment to the Road Map and the two-state solution as well as its commitment to negotiations for a final status agreement. He qualified this by stating that further steps, even in connection with the Road Map, could not be undertaken by Israel "absent the emergence of a Palestinian partner committed to peace, democratic reform and the fight against terror. *Once such a Palestinian partner emerges, the Israeli government will perform its obligations as called for in the Road Map* . . ." [Emphasis mine].

A year later such a partner did emerge, in the form of Abu Mazen. At one point, Sharon even agreed that this was a partner,[4] meeting with him under Jordanian auspices at Sharm al-Sheikh in February 2005 in order to reach new understandings. These included, once again, promises to release prisoners, hand back some of the reoccupied Palestinian towns (from Area A), lift roadblocks, and the like, along with mutual Palestinian and Israeli commitments to end all violence and military action.[5] Yet despite the advent of a partner, plus these new understandings, and even the disengagement, the Palestinians' "fight against terror" would remain the qualification and requirement to be defined by the government of Israel. A return to negotiations to which Sharon had committed Israel would depend, apparently, on that definition, unless President Bush and the Quartet exercised their prerogative to determine "performance" in the Road Map. For its part, Israel viewed itself, according to Sharon, in "a pre-Road Map stage."[6]

CHAPTER FOURTEEN

Conclusions—Is There a Plan for Peace?

The failure of the Oslo Accords, underlined and ingrained in the minds of both publics by the tragic violence that followed, led to the belief among many Israelis and Palestinians that no agreed peace plan could ever be achieved. Yet in fact there was an evolution in thinking and positions over the course of the difficult intervening years from Oslo to the Disengagement. Beginning with the mutual recognition of both peoples, including the Israeli use of the word "Palestinian" instead of simply "Arab," that resulted from Oslo, a sea change in the attitudes of both peoples actually took place. The idea of the two-state solution that had begun as a slogan of a small communist fringe back in the early 1970s and adopted by the PLO in 1988 became by 2004 a declared policy goal of the Government of Israel—a government led by the right-wing Likud party and a right-wing prime minister, Ariel Sharon. The same government acknowledged that Israel's presence in the Gaza Strip was "occupation," and Sharon himself acknowledged the same status regarding the West Bank, despite the traditional official position that this was merely "disputed" territory. Beginning with Oslo, and compounded by another right-wing prime minister and government in the Wye River Memorandum (1998), the idea of retaining all of Greater Israel (the Land of Israel or western Eretz Israel) was dealt a fatal blow. This was made abundantly clear with Sharon's precedent-setting evacuation of twenty-five well-established settlements and total withdrawal from the Gaza Strip. Concepts such as a "viable" Palestinian state and the need for "contiguity" became standard phrases, to say nothing of "territorial compromise" or "land for peace" which once had been anathema for right-wing governments. Even the question of how much land Israel might annex in the end underwent a sea of change. The 4 June 1967 line became a recognized guideline, dictating, for example, alterations even to the demarcation of the separation barrier, bringing that barrier closer to the 1967 line (thanks to the Israeli High Court and international, especially American, pressure). Yet this would still not represent a satisfactory solution from the Palestinian point of view, especially with its inclusion of all of East Jerusalem and surrounding areas into Israel (including thousands of Palestinians and with no territorial compensation to the Palestinians, i.e. swaps). But if the line of the barrier were to become the border, it would mean Israeli annexation of only roughly nine to ten percent of the West Bank—far closer to a solution than any right-wing government of Israel had ever approached.[1] Were it just a question of precedents, the government under Barak had actually agreed to concede still more when it accepted the now defunct Clinton Parameters—with their approximately nine percent equal land swap idea. In any case, at least in terms of the principle of territorial compromise, even right-wing Israel had come a long way. Gone were the ideas of Greater Israel and even claims of the need for territorial "strategic depth" for Israel's security, as demography began to replace territory in Israeli strategic thinking.

The Palestinian position also evolved in a way. In addition to accepting Israel's right to exist and the two-state solution, with a Palestinian state on just twenty-two percent of Mandated Palestine, the Palestinians agreed to negotiate the 1967 borders in the form of land swaps. Moreover, and implied by the swaps, they accepted the idea of settlement blocs to be retained by Israel, along with other border adjustments. They also seemed to have accepted the continued presence of Israel in the form of early warning stations and a presence on the eastern (Jordan) border for a limited period of time, and at various stages of the negotiations, they were ready to permit Israeli use of roads in case of emergency, along with IDF training in Palestinian airspace. With their belated acceptance of the now defunct Clinton Parameters, the Palestinians actually accepted all of these measures along with demilitarization of the Palestinian state.

Both sides agreed to an international presence, and in the Road Map, but particularly in the Disengagement Plan, Israel took unprecedented steps in the direction of third-party involvement. A change in the American position took place as well. Despite Bush's pronouncements regarding the refugee issue and the settlements (the latter being in fact no more than the settlement bloc idea), the US President went further than any of his predecessors, including Clinton, in officially adopting the two-state solution.

On all of the above issues and possibly more (such as water, economic relations, and use of airspace), most of the Palestinian and Israeli negotiators believed that agreement had been or could be reached. Indeed, the Geneva Accord was viewed by many as the proof of this, even if each of the specific solutions it proffered needed further modification.

What remained were the two issues that had assumed center place over the period from Oslo to the Disengagement: the problems of Jerusalem and the refugees. These appeared to replace in importance even the traditional concerns of Israel over security, and they seemed impossible to resolve. Even moderate Israeli observers, including former negotiators and persons on the left, became skeptical when it came to these two issues. In the past, they had believed Palestinian leaders who had claimed that compromise on the refugee issue was possible but, it appeared, subsequently changed their positions— either because they, the Palestinians, saw that they would not be able to achieve public support for such a compromise or, in a less charitable analysis, because they had never been sincere in the first place. This Palestinian turnabout, or at least what was perceived by Israel as such, could be seen in Camp David. Similarly, there were definitely different degrees of willingness on the part of Israelis to make even a symbolic compromise on the refugee issue. What some Israeli leaders could accept regarding acknowledgement of Resolution 194 was denied by others who demanded not only explicit renunciation of the right of return but also recognition of the Jewish right to—and Jewish character of—the State of Israel as prerequisites for even opening new negotiations. Indeed the right of return seemed to become, for both peoples, the litmus test for the very possibility of ever resolving the conflict. Jerusalem was added to this primarily in symbolic terms. The Palestinian challenge to the Jewish claim to the Temple Mount was interpreted by Israelis as part of the same historic and perpetual rejection of the Jews' right to Israel altogether—and therefore existence as a Jewish state. In this way, the two issues became connected, emotionally and symbolically, even for those for whom religious sites such at the Temple Mount held no importance whatsoever. There was a certain similarity in the connection for the Palestinians as well. As early as the 1920s, Palestinian riots had erupted over what had been perceived as a Jewish threat to the Muslim holy site of the Haram al-Sharif. Excavations and construction in this area are not merely physical endeavors; they are potentially fatal blows to the spiritual and historic presence of each side. It is in this context, therefore, that the sovereignty issue must be seen—going far beyond mundane matters of authority or control. Given this context, including the connection with the refugee issue, there are those who believe that the interests of the two sides are incompatible, and as a result a permanent peace agreement is not possible. However, in the case that there is a will for peace, then there would also be the understanding that these apparently irreconcilable interests must be dealt with in a different way. What evolved in the course of the elaboration of the various proposals was exactly this. The result was perhaps the only logical solution: a trade-off, as in the Clinton Parameters, the Geneva Accord, and to a lesser degree in the Ayalon-Nusseibeh Declaration, together with statements about the legitimacy of each of both peoples in Jerusalem and in their own states. That there was official thinking in this direction might be evidenced by Abu Mazen's efforts to persuade refugees that there was little to no hope to return, coupled with comments among Palestinians about the need for "development" within the refugee camps[2]—as distinct from the historic position of maintaining the physical and socioeconomic status quo of the camps in order to strengthen the case for return.

The sad truth is that both Palestinians and Israelis have come to realize, particularly since Oslo, that a solution, which would be the end of the conflict, can only come about with something like the above compromises and in all likelihood the critical Jerusalem/refugees tradeoff as well. This is a sad truth because the two societies could have avoided all the killings and hardships before finally reaching what has been clear for so long. Yet, many Israelis, though not a majority, believe that Israel will not have to make such concessions, but rather will be able to hold onto control of the West Bank, including East Jerusalem, permanently, even if it means periodic battles against rebelling Palestinians. There are also minority-held ideas connected with population transfers or border changes that would place parts of Israel inhabited by Palestinian citizens of Israel under the rule of Palestine (or Jordan) in exchange for Israeli annexation of the bulk of the West Bank. Similarly there are Palestinians who continue to believe that all of Mandated Palestine will be recovered at some point, if not through terror or military victory, then by time and demographics. According to one perception, Palestinians will soon constitute a majority as distinct from Jews in the areas controlled by Israel today, from the Jordan River to the Mediterranean Sea, and this situation will eventually lead to branding Israel an apartheid state. Since this would be intolerable to the international community, the result, some believe, would then be an enforced bi-national state in the whole area and the demise of the State of Israel. Whatever the reality or feasibility of any of these ideas, they have remained minority views on both sides even throughout the disappointments and trials of the period since Oslo, and even with the extremist acts on both sides, the rise of Hamas and the belief that there is "no partner."

The emergence of leaders on both sides, Abu Mazen and a right-wing leader, Ariel Sharon, who both openly rejected all of these ideas and advocated the two-state solution—however different their conceptions of this may have been—was a sign of the progress, not regression, that has taken place since, and in many ways because of, Oslo. One may add to this the war weariness of both societies, along with pressing economic interests, plus the successful evacuation of Israeli settlements in 2005, the increased involvement of the international community, and American advocacy of the two-state solution and the Arab League's willingness to normalize relations with an Israel living alongside an independent Palestine. Balanced against the admittedly serious negative consequences of the failed peace process, and even bearing in mind the continued Israeli expansion of settlements and the fragility of Abu Mazen's leadership, a case can nonetheless be made for the possibility that the two sides will opt for realism—leaving the issue of trust to a later stage—and adopt something quite close to the peace plans that have emerged.

Epilogue

A salient feature of the Arab-Israeli conflict and Israeli-Palestinian relations has been the absence of a "status quo" for any lengthy period of time. Despite the endurance of some of the issues, the political environment as well as the situation on the ground is almost constantly in flux—sometimes bouleversement. The 2006 elections in the Palestinian Authority and in Israel were both examples. The election of Hamas, replacing Fatah as the ruling party in the Palestinian Authority, brought to power a group officially and explicitly unwilling to recognize or negotiate with the state of Israel, or to accept territorial compromise. Unlike the nationalist, basically secular Fatah, Hamas is part of the Muslim Brotherhood movement, aspiring to an Islamic state in all of Palestine. And in Israel, the change of leadership brought about by Sharon's stroke, which brought to power his successor Ehud Olmert, led to a coalition government elected on a platform of unilateralism. While this was a policy that Sharon too might have pursued,[1] his successor, as leader of the party Sharon had just created, openly declared his intention unilaterally to set Israel's permanent borders. This was to be accomplished in what he called a "convergence" (later "realignment") of the settlements on the West Bank.

Offering the rationale of the demographic problem connected with holding on to all of the territory and the absence of a partner for negotiations (stated even before the election of Hamas), Israel would evacuate a large number of settlements on the West Bank, moving their residents into the settlement blocs that would be preserved as indicated by the route of the separation barrier—the latter to become Israel's border. The full plan was not clear; a number of elements were announced but an official, detailed plan was not presented. The two most important and unclear points of the plan were the actual border intended and the status of the evacuated areas. There were rumors, and Olmert had said in the past that some ninety percent of the West Bank would be on the other side of the border, that is, the border would be roughly the line of the fence as officially approved together with the changes demanded by the Supreme Court.[2] Yet, the inclusion of the settlement blocs (in which construction continued, leaving their final size far from clear) and specifically settlements such as Ariel, along with planned expansions beyond Jerusalem, for example, all indicated a border that would annex far more territory of the West Bank. Moreover, Israel would keep certain areas deemed militarily important, including but not only the Jordan Valley. Nor was it clear that Israel would in fact actually withdraw from the remainder of the West Bank, for while settlements were to be dismantled, the Israeli military would maintain security responsibility (as in the case of the four settlements evacuated in the northern West Bank under the August 2006 Disengagement), in their place, something akin to area B of the Oslo Accords. None of these elements was entirely clear, however, as the plan was yet to be finally drawn much less approved by the government. Indeed, in response to international, including American, protestations of opposition to Israel unilaterally drawing its borders, Foreign Minister Tzipi Livni told the World Economic Forum in May 2006 that while the line of the fence was determined by security considerations, Israel's permanent borders would be decided in final status negotiations.[3] Further, also in response to international, especially American, and Arab (Egyptian, Jordanian) opposition, Olmert repeatedly committed Israel to negotiating with the Palestinians and undertaking the "convergence" only if these talks failed. The government set preconditions for such negotiations, the same conditions the international community (the Quartet) set for speaking with the newly elected Hamas government. These were recognition of Israel,[4] abandonment of the use of terror and acceptance of previously negotiated agreements and obligations. There was little expectation that Hamas would accept these conditions, but there were also few if any signs that Olmert was seeking to speak with any alternative Palestinian leadership. In talks with European and Arab leaders, Olmert committed to opening some form of talks with Abu Mazen, still President of the Palestine Authority and Chairman of the PLO, and he proclaimed continued interest in the Road Map—demanding as in the past that the Palestinians fulfill their part of the first phase of the Road Map before Israel would proceed on that track or, apparently, enter any negotiations. But few in Israel believed that the government led by Olmert intended to undertake anything but unilateral steps. The irony of the situation was that an apparent willingness of Israel to give up most of the West Bank—perhaps a step genuinely intended to extricate Israel from the occupied territories—was not perceived internationally, nor by many domestically, as a step that would in fact end the occupation and certainly not one that would end the conflict.

Yet the election of Hamas appeared to leave no other positive alternative. Indeed, there was once again the threat of large-scale Israeli military action, for although the new Palestinian government, under Prime Minister Ismail Haniye, maintained the self-imposed ceasefire of Hamas, it did nothing to prevent or stop daily firing of shells from Gaza into Israel and occasional terror attacks. Israel accompanied and responded to this low-level violence with further assassinations, shelling and bombing by the IDF. At the same time, both Israel and the international community[5] related to Hamas as a terror organization and therefore maintained a strict boycott on the Palestinian Authority, preventing economic, financial and virtually any kind of aid to reach the Palestinians, with the exception of some humanitarian aid provided through very limited channels. The goal presumably was the collapse of the Hamas government, which, unable to pay salaries to the vast numbers of persons working for the Authority, including the security forces of the previous government, faced violent clashes with unpaid Fatah personnel and others in Gaza and with rival security groups in the West Bank as well.

This apparent unilateralism on both sides need not, however, be seen as either permanent or as a sign of total stalemate. Neither the Israeli nor the Palestinian elections was a rejection of the two-state solution or even of negotiations. On the Palestinian side, the election victory of Hamas was to some degree the result of the voting system rather than majority support for the movement. More to the point, however, was the fact that the vote for Hamas was to a large degree a protest vote against the corruption and failures of Fatah. Oslo was considered one of these failures, while Hamas was credited with getting Israel out of Gaza (since there had been no negotiations for the disengagement Abu Mazen and Fatah could hardly take credit for that event). Yet, a poll conducted a few months after the elections strongly suggested that the policies of Hamas were not necessarily the reason for Palestinians' votes. The poll indicated continued, even slightly increased support for Hamas, and a decline in support for Fatah, but at the same time, majority support both for a two-state solution and negotiations with Israel.[6] Apparently confident that these are in fact the positions of the Palestinian public, and strengthened by the growing inability of Hamas to govern due to the difficulties caused by the international boycott, Abu Mazen challenged his Hamas Prime Minister, Ismail Haniye, to accept the principle of the two-state solution, whether as expressed in the Arab League Resolution or in the more vague formulations of a letter composed in May 2006 by Palestinian security prisoners in Israeli jails—including leading Hamas detainees.[7] Abu Mazen called for a referendum to be held on the letter, known as the Prisoners' Document (which also called for a unity government between Fatah and Hamas) unless Hamas agreed. Negotiations began between the two to find a formula for acceptance of the Prisoners' Letter, along with possible Hamas admission to the PLO, and the creation of a national unity government, although violent clashes continued locally between Fatah and Hamas.

On the Israeli side, the elections in March 2006 were in fact the first time almost all of the parties standing for election accepted the two-state solution, including, most significantly, the leading party: Sharon's creation, Kadima, composed of figures from both left and right-wing parties, mainly from his own Likud. Indeed what was left of the Likud was almost totally decimated electorally, along with the extreme right wing nationalist-religious bloc. Public sentiment in Israel remained in favor of the two-state solution—but still maintained the "no partner" conviction. Nonetheless, polls continued to indicate majority support for negotiations, with contradictory findings regarding support for Olmert's convergence plan.[8] Indeed even within the government coalition there were differences of opinion—from right and left. Outside the government, voices could be heard in favor of negotiating, seriously, with Abu Mazen, either in his capacity as President of the Palestinian Authority (even if Prime Minister Haniye and his government themselves refused to conduct negotiations), or as head of the PLO, which was the organization that was authorized to negotiate as the legitimate representative of the Palestinian people (outside as well as inside the area of the Palestinian Authority).

Indeed the alternatives, at the time of this writing, appear to be 1) Israeli acceptance of Abu Mazen (possibly acting with Hamas approval) as a negotiating partner; 2) Israeli acceptance of Hamas as a negotiating partner without preconditions; 3) Hamas acceptance of Israel's preconditions for negotiations (probably resulting in a split between moderate Hamas elements inside the occupied territories and the militant Hamas outside); 4) continued Hamas resistance to negotiations; 5) continued Israeli unilateralism. Given the ever-changing dynamics of the Israeli-Palestinian conflict, still more alternatives may well be possible. Moreover, both sides appear to be in a state of flux: a delicately balanced Israeli coalition government divided over a plan yet to be finally formulated; a two-headed Palestinian Authority locked in a power struggle over a policy that may determine its survival.

Postscript

As this book goes to press in the summer of 2006, the ever-changing dynamics that are characteristic of the conflict intervened once again in the form of the Israel-Hezbollah war. The tragic events of this summer, including Israeli military's move back into the Gaza Strip, highlighted once again the urgent need for negotiations and resolution of the conflict. On the positive side, these events not only spawned Israeli agreement to an international force (in southern Lebanon) but also generated proposals for an international conference to press for a comprehensive settlement. In addition the war led Olmert to abandon his unilateral plans. Depending upon the outcomes, these developments could provide promising elements for achieving peace in Israel and Palestine.

Galia Golan
Israel
August 2006

Notes

Chapter One

1. The most thorough history of the conflict is Benny Morris, *Righteous Victims: A History of the Zionist-Arab Conflict*, Knopf, New York, 1999. See also Charles Smith, *Palestine and the Arab-Israeli Conflict*, Bedford/St. Martin's, Boston, 2004; Alan Dowty, *Israel/Palestine*, Polity, Cambridge, Massachusetts, 2005.

2. Palestine was the name given by the Greeks apparently because of the Philistines, a sea people who settled and dominated the area around 1200 BC. For the Jews this was part of the Kingdoms of Israel and Judah that were eventually created by the Hebrews after they too reached the land around 1200 BC. After their expulsion by the Romans in the second century AD, Jews referred to Palestine as part of the Land of Israel (Eretz Israel), the latter having stretched from the Mediterranean Sea to the Euphrates River.

3. Israel had not in fact intended to take the West Bank when this war broke out. The government contacted King Hussein twice on the morning of

5 June 1967 with assurances that Israel had no plan to strike Jordan and urged him to remain outside the war despite his recent defense pact with Egypt.

4. Previous Labor governments had also established settlements, but on a far smaller scale and without the intention of retaining the bulk of the territory. (For this period, see Gershon Gorenberg, *The Accidental Empire: Israel and the Birth of the Settlements, 1967–1977*, Times Books, New York, 2006. See also Akiva Eldar and Idit Zertal, *Adonei Haaretz (Lords of the Land: The Settlers and the State of Israel 1967–2004)*, Kinneret, Zmora-Bitan, Dvir Publishing House, Or Yehuda, Israel, 2004).

5. Dealing with cultural aspects, for example, see Tamara Coffman Wittes (ed.), *How Israelis and Palestinians Negotiate*, United States Institute of Peace, Washington, 2005; also Shibley Telhami, "Beyond Resolution? The Palestinian-Israeli Conflict" in Chester Crocker, Fen Osler Hampson and Pamela Aall (eds.), *Grasping the Nettle: Analyzing Cases of Intractable Conflict*, United States Institute of Peace, Washington, 2005, pp. 357–374; on negotiating patterns, Laura Zittrani Eisenberg and Neil Caplan, *Negotiating Arab-Israeli Peace*, Indiana University Press, Bloomington, 1998. On Oslo, Geoffrey Watson, *The Oslo Accords: International Law and the Israeli-Palestinian Peace Agreements*, Oxford University Press, London, 2000 (although these were not "peace agreements") or Uri Savir, *The Process*, Vintage Books, N.Y., 1998; Mahmoud Abbas (Abu Mazen), *Through Secret Channels*, Garnet Publishing, Reading, 1995; Ahmed Qurie ('Abu Al'). *From Oslo to Jerusalem: The Palestinian Story of the Secret Negotiations*, I.B. Tauris, London, 2006. On Camp David and subsequent negotiations, see notes in Chapter 3.

Chapter Two

1. See Galia Golan, *The Soviet Union and the Palestine Liberation Organization: An Uneasy Alliance*, Praeger Publishers, N.Y., 1980.

2. See Galia Golan, *Moscow and the Middle East: New Thinking on Regional Conflict*, The Royal Institute of International Affairs, London, 1992; Ga-

lia Golan, *Soviet Policies in the Middle East from World War II to Gorbachev*, Cambridge University Press, Cambridge, 1990; or Robert Freedman, *Moscow and the Middle East: Soviet Policy Since the Invasion of Afghanistan*, Cambridge University Press, N. Y., 1991.

3. Viz., the King Hussein-Yasser Arafat Agreement of February 1985.

4. Yezid Sayigh, *Armed Struggle and Search for State*, Oxford University Press, Washington, D.C., 1999, p. 624.

5. See Jacob Shamir and Michal Shamir, *The Anatomy of Public Opinion*, University of Michigan Press, 2000 and Galia Golan, "Israel and Palestinian Statehood," in Winston Van Horne (ed.), *Global Convulsions: Race, Ethnicity and Nationalism at the End of the Twentieth Century*, State University of New York Press, N.Y., 1997, pp. 169–188.

6. Part of Clinton's commitment to his anti-Iraq coalition in 1990–1991 and to Gorbachev was a promise to deal with the Arab-Israeli conflict immediately after the war. The Madrid Conference of 1991 was the outcome of this. The conference met for just two days and then broke up into a number of multilateral committees on various issues. Israel did not permit a PLO delegation, but PLO (unofficially) affiliated Palestinians participated as part of the Jordanian delegation. Most noteworthy was Syrian participation for the first time. The lack of progress in the multilaterals led to the decision to open the Oslo track.

7. Israeli writer Amos Oz once characterized the situation in the Oslo period as one in which the doctor woke up the patient in the middle of an operation and asked him how he felt. Until completed, or even knowing the final result, the process could hardly be judged.

8. Resolution 242 does not state how much or which of the territories occupied in 1967 and Israeli governments have interpreted the clause quite freely, but looked at from the point of view of the traditional PLO position (liberation of all of Palestine west of the Jordan River) acceptance of 242 meant acceptance of the limitation to the West Bank and Gaza, i.e., the mini-state.

9. Few were to notice that Rabin's letter referred to the "Palestinian" Liberation Movement rather than the correct (but for Israel at the time unacceptable) name of the organization "the Palestine Liberation

Organization." Israel was and remains unwilling officially to speak of "Palestine" because of the territorial implications.

10. In 1975 Kissinger had promised Israel not to open any dialogue with the PLO unless it recognized Israel's right to exist and renounced the use of terror. Washington reportedly actually dictated such wording to Arafat for his 1988 press conference after the PLO leader had used more vague terms in his speech to the specially held session UNGA in Geneva and in the PNC's resolution, both referred to above.

11. Similar to the concept of a Framework of Principles worked out before a final agreement, for example, between Egypt and Israel in 1978.

12. Uri Savir, *The Process*, Vintage Books, New York, 1998, p. 72.

13. The Gaza-Jericho agreement, for example, had used the term "withdrawal."

14. Even Rabin was to declare that "no dates are sacred" (*New York Times*, 14 December 1993).

15. By a vote of 504 for abrogation, 54 against, 214 abstentions at the PNC meeting 24 April 1996.

16. Always a sensitive issue, a perceived threat to the Haram al-Sharif was the trigger for the 1929 Palestinian riots and later, in 2000, the Al-Aksa Intifada.

17. In the Gaza Disengagement, an international presence was allowed, but only in areas that Israel claimed were no longer under occupation. Originally TIP was to be 400 persons; TIPH consists of just 71, with no authority to intervene but only to observe and report problems or disturbances.

18. Shimon Peres called it "the most important change in the last 100 years" (CNN, 30 April 1996).

19. After the previous withdrawal, the Palestinians controlled 2.9% of the West Bank (area A) and had partial (civic) control over twenty-four percent (area B) and Israel controlled seventy-three percent (area C). Had the redeployments of the memorandum been implemented, the breakdown would have become: area A 17.1%; area B 21.8%, and area C 61.1%.

20. Benny Morris, *Righteous Victims*, Knopf, N.Y., 1999, p. 647; Dennis Ross, *The Missing Peace*, Farrar Strauss & Giroux, N.Y., 2004, p. 412.

21. Ross, p. 375.
22. How, was not explained. This was a compromise since the Palestinians rejected the idea of the Americans actually collecting the weapons. Ross, p. 425.
23. The Palestinians participating in the committee insisted upon looking at Israeli incitement as well.
24. Bill Clinton (*My Life*, Vintage Books, New York, 2005, p. 818) stated that the Palestinians trusted CIA director George Tenet.
25. 14 December 1999.
26. The "Sharm-el-Sheikh Memorandum on Implementation Timeline of Outstanding Commitments of Agreements Signed and the Resumption of Permanent Status Negotiations," 4 September 1999.

Chapter Three

1. Clinton; Ross; Charles Enderlin, *Shattered Dreams*, Other Press, N.Y. 2002; Shlomo Ben Ami, *A Front Without A Rearguard* (Hebrew), Yediot Aharonot Books, Tel Aviv, 2004; Gilead Sher, *Just Beyond Reach* (Hebrew), Yediot Aharonot Books, 2001; PLO Negotiating Team website (www.nad-plo.org); Akram Haniyeh, "The Camp David Paper," *Journal of Palestine Studies*, Vol. 30, No. 2, 2001, pp. 75–97; Yossi Beilin, *The Path to Geneva*, RDV Books, N.Y., 2004; Danny Rubinstein, Robert Malley, Hussein Agha, Ehud Barak, Benny Morris, *Camp David 2000: Rashamon Camp David* (Hebrew), Neged Haruach Publishers, Tel Aviv, 2003; Ghassan Khatib, "Camp David: An Exit Strategy for Barak," Bitterlemons, Edition 26, July 15, 2002 (www.bitterlemons.org) and more. Of these many good accounts, the best and most succinct analysis is probably that of Hussein Agha and Robert Malley, "Camp David: The Tragedy of Errors," *New York Review of Books*, Vol. 48, No. 13, August 9, 2001.
2. Ross, p. 688.
3. Ben Ami, p. 187; Ross, pp. 688–689.
4. Ben-Ami, p. 171.
5. An Israeli government decision of 26 June 1967 tripled the size of mu-

nicipal (West) Jerusalem by adding 71,000 dunams of land—6,000 from East Jerusalem and the rest from twenty-eight villages around Jerusalem in the West Bank.

6. Col. ret. Ephraim Lavie (one of the advisors to the Israeli team), "The Road Map: Political Resolution Instead of National Narrative Confrontation," *Palestine-Israel Journal*, Vol. 10, No .4, 2003, pp. 83–91.

7. Ephraim Yaar and Tamar Hermann, *Peace Index*, July 2000 (Tami Steinmetz Center for Peace Research, Tel Aviv University). During the talks, however, the encouraging sign had been that leaked concessions regarding Jerusalem—previously a taboo topic—had not aroused much of a response.

8. Most of this version may be found in the PLO Negotiating Team's "Camp David Peace Proposal of July 2000," www.nad-plo.org. See also, Mustafa Barghouti, "Generous to Whom," *Al Ahram* weekly on-line, 10–16 May 2001, Issue No. 533 (*www.weekly.abram.org*).

9. See for example, Khatib.

Chapter Four

1. Ben-Ami reported what he claims were the Palestinian reservations, p. 414.

2. Clinton (p. 944) said Arafat finally agreed, a year and one half later, well after the elections of Sharon and Bush—and well into the Intifada.

Chapter Five

1. Both these claims in Enderlin, p. 344.

2. EU Special Representative to the Middle East Peace Process, Amb. Miguel Moratinos' "non-paper" available at www.ariga.com/treaties/taba/shtml.

3. Sher, for example, minimizes what was accomplished; Beilin is far more positive.

4. The talks were even suspended for two days when two visiting Israelis were killed in a West Bank village.
5. Enderlin, p. 342; Beilin, p. 243.
6. Beilin, p. 246.
7. Unresolved were questions such as the status of the Latrun salient, the Maaleh Adumim settlement city, and other Jewish settlements on the outskirts of Jerusalem.
8. As discussed, though not agreed, in earlier talks, the Palestinians would have the Muslim, Christian and part of the Armenian quarters, and Israel would retain the Jewish and part of the Armenian quarter.
9. Yossi Beilin, *The Path to Geneva*, RDV Books, N. Y., 2004.
10. The assumptions were that the refugees in the West Bank and Gaza were automatically part of the Palestinian state, those in Jordan were already citizens of Jordan, and those in Syria were able to work and live there. Therefore, the main concern was for the180,000 to 220,000 refugees in Lebanon.

Chapter Six

1. The committee was the result of a Middle East Peace Summit Clinton held in Sharm el-Sheikh 17 October 2000 after the outbreak of the Intifada, but before his Parameters and Taba. Egypt, Jordan, the U.S., the EU and the UN participated along with Israel and Palestinian Authority.
2. Letter from the Prime Minister's Office, 15 May 2001, signed by Dan Naveh accompanying the "Comment of the Government of Israel on the Report of the Sharm el-Sheikh Fact-Finding Committee."
3. Letter of 15 May 2001 signed by Minister of Culture and Information Yasser Abed Rabbo accompanying the "Official Response of the Palestine Liberation Organization to the Final Report of the Sharm el-Sheikh Fact-Finding Committee."
4. *Ha'aretz*, 14 June 2001, and JMCC website,www.jmcc.org/documents/ Tenet.htm. "Second US 'Joint Goals' Proposal," www.jmcc.org/ documents/zinnipaper.htm

Chapter Seven

1. Nearly twenty years earlier, the Arab League had accepted a proposal by King Fahd of Saudi Arabia, known as the Fez Plan, quite similar to the new initiative, without, however, specifically mentioning Israel or granting normalization to Israel. See Bernard Reich (ed.), *Arab-Israeli Conflict and Conciliation*, Praeger, N. Y., 1995, pp. 179–180. Prince Abdullah's speech to the Arab League after the outbreak of the Intifada contained sentiments similar to those now expressed in the initiative (first publicized in a *New York Times*, 17 February article by Tom Friedman).
2. An additional change was the specific inclusion of Syria and territories in southern Lebanon in the post-67 occupied territories to be evacuated.
3. The Resolution was in fact reaffirmed by the Arab League at its meeting in Khartoum, May 2006.
4. Only Syria, at the time a member of the Council, abstained. There were no votes against the resolution.

Chapter Eight

1. The White House, "The President Meets With Congressional Leaders," 2 October 2001, www.whitehouse.gov/news/releases.
2. The White House, "President Bush and Prime Minister Sharon Discuss the Middle East," 7 February 2002, www.whitehouse.gov/news/releases.
3. The White House, "President Bush Calls for New Palestinian Leadership," 24 June 2002, www.whitehouse.gov/news/releases.

Chapter Nine

1. A draft of the Road Map was actually published 20 December 2002 and the later official version did not differ from it. However, the dates for

each phase were not changed, causing a certain distortion of the original intentions particularly regarding Phase I.

2. Resolution 181 of 1947 was never mentioned in these contexts even though it provided for two states. The reason was that the territorial lines of that resolution were perceived by Israel, and generally, as no longer relevant. They had been superseded by the armistice lines that ended the war in 1949, becoming the de facto or unofficial borders of Israel, referred to as the 4 June 1967 lines.

3. As noted, the dates were not changed when the official publication was delayed. It is unlikely that the original intention had been that the Phase I would last just one month.

4. The Task Force created by the Quartet included Norway, Japan, the World Bank and the IMF.

5. Ms. Catherine Bertini, Personal Humanitarian Envoy of the Secretary-General, *Mission Report*, 11–19 August 2002. The Road Map called for implementation of the recommendations addressed to the Palestinians as well as to Israel.

6. Eldar and Zertal, p. 229.

7. On the whole, the demarcation of the separation barrier was to incorporate all of East Jerusalem and much of the surrounding area, plus settlement blocs the final size of which remained undetermined, all beyond the 1967 ("green") line and leaving thousands of Palestinians west of the fence. See map, p. 134.

8. Hanan Ashrawi, for example, called for "direct third party supervision and viable involvement with a mandate for arbitration and accountability." (*Palestine Chronicle*, 1 November 2002, during discussions of the draft of the Road Map).

9. "Conclusions of the London Meeting on Supporting the Palestinian Authority," British Embassy Bulletin, 1 March 2005 (www.britbot.de/en/news).

10. All of the objections were published in *Ha'aretz*, 28 May 2003.

11. Ephraim Yaar and Tamar Hermann, *Peace Index: April 2003* (Tami Steinmetz Center for Peace Research, Tel Aviv University).

Chapter Ten

1. The group grew out of the Israeli-Palestinian Peace Coalition created by Beilin and Peace Now immediately after the election of Sharon, with Abed Rabbo, Hanan Ashrawi and others on the Palestinian side.
2. So called because of the support rendered the group by the Swiss government. In time, the Accord came to be known as the Geneva Initiative (to indicate its unofficial status).
3. Reconciliation was mentioned in only one other place, in part of a sentence on the tasks of the joint committee for Jerusalem.
4. Maha abu Dayyeh Shamas quoted in Galia Golan, "The Role of Women in Conflict Resolution," *Palestine-Israel Journal*, Vol. 11, No. 2, 2004, pp. 92–96.
5. Following Camp David Arafat had made a statement to the effect that the Jews had no religious connection to the Temple Mount/Haram al-Sharif, as evidenced by the fact that Jews did not even pray there. Of course he failed to mention (or perhaps understand) that religious Jews were forbidden to do so, and some Jews ("Cohen-im," i.e., those descending from the Priests) were forbidden even to enter the site, both for religious reasons.
6. Ghassan Khatib, "Actualizing Peace," *Bitterlemons*, Edition 39, October 27, 2003, www.bitterlemons.org.
7. For a more detailed analysis of the response, see Galia Golan, "Plans for Israeli-Palestinian Peace," *Middle East Policy*, Vol. 11, No. 1, 2004, pp. 38–51.

Chapter Eleven

1. The fact that Ami Ayalon subsequently joined the Labor Party and was elected to the Knesset hurt this appeal, although the campaign did continue on a smaller scale.
2. According to the official website of The Peoples' Voice, www.mifkad.org.il, 18 August 2005. By August 2006 the website showed an increase of 47 Israeli signatures and no additional Palestinian signatures.

Chapter Twelve

1. In *Ha'aretz*, 3 February 2004 he was quoted on three West Bank settlements, but later it became four. These were isolated settlements with relatively few inhabitants, although they covered a territory far greater in size than the settlements in Gaza. As it eventually became clear, however, Israel would not be handing this area over to the PA but rather simply taking down the settlements.

2. It must be remembered that the separation barrier (fence/wall) was not even initially supported by Sharon much less part of his conception for the future. And even in its settler-influenced expansionist routing, it was not necessarily the line Sharon would have liked to see since it might in fact incorporate more Palestinians and less land than he perhaps would have preferred. Presumably for this reason, after four years of construction not even half of the barrier had been completed.

3. According to international law, "Territory is considered occupied when it is actually placed under the authority of the hostile army. The occupation extends only to the territory where such authority has been established and can be exercised" (The Hague Regulations Respecting the Laws and Customs of War on Land, article 42, as cited by Prof. Ruth Lapidoth in "Unity Does Not Require Uniformity" *Bitterlemons*, Edition 30, August 22, 2005, www.bitterlemons.org).

4. Gaza's own water supply was polluted by seawater and sewage; clean water was purchased from Israel, which derived its water from aquifers located in the area between the Jordan River and the Mediterranean Sea (i.e., including the West Bank). See Amira Hass, "Where Will the Water Come From?," *Ha'aretz*, 1 September 2005.

5. *Bitterlemons*, Edition 30, August 22, 2005 addressed this issue.

6. The G-8 committed to three billion dollars, in addition to other sums promised the World Bank and the international community.

7. Neither the seaport nor the airport was in fact permitted following the disengagement.

8. As a result of the behind-the-scenes coordination with the PA there was total quiet from the Palestinians during the actual disengagement. After much discussion, it was also agreed that Israel would totally dismantle

the evacuated settlements, while some of the commercial facilities were transferred to the Palestinians through private transactions.

9. During the Camp David negotiations in 1978, when then PM Begin balked at the Egyptian demand to evacuate the settlements, then Agricultural Minister Sharon, who earlier in the peace process had actually begun the building of new settlements in the Sinai, telephoned Begin and told him to agree (William Quandt, *Camp David: Peacemaking and Politics*, Brookings Institution, Washington, D.C., 1986, p. 241).

10. Peace Now commissioned "Settler Attitude" studies in July 2002, 2003 and 2004. The findings may be seen at www.peacenow.org.il.

Chapter Thirteen

1. Letter reprinted in *Ha'aretz*, "Disengagement Special Magazine," 15 August 2005, pp. 61–62.

2. Ha'aretz, p. 60.

3. *Ha'aretz*., p. 61.

4. Interview in *Yediot Ahronot*, 12 August 2005.

5. Although it is often referred to, the "Sharm el-Sheikh Understandings," of 8 February 2005, was never published. Sharon and Abu Mazen's speeches were published but contained no details beyond the agreement to stop all acts of violence and a Sharon promise to release prisoners. Sharon's speech, Israel Ministry of Foreign Affairs site, www.mfa.gov and Abu Mazen's speech, www.electronicintifada.net.

6. See Yonatan Touval, "Epitaph for a Road Map," *Ha'aretz*, 23 March 2006, for the connection between Disengagement and the Road Map in the eyes of Israel.

Chapter Fourteen

1. The original demarcation (see map p. 134) approved by the Government in October 2003 would have annexed eighteen percent of the West Bank.

Following the April 2004 Supreme Court decision, the new line approved by the Government in February 2005 allowed for nine percent. An eastern fence (in the Jordan Valley) was never brought for Government approval, mainly because of American objections. If it had been or were approved, it would add another thirty-five percent of the land to Israel. The nine percent includes East Jerusalem though not necessarily settlements or outposts that might be added to the settlement blocs and areas still under consideration.

2. Walid Salem referred to this in "New Trends in the Palestinian Refugee Problem," at the conference *Looking Beyond Regional Crisis*, Amman, 22 March 2004 (unpublished paper).

Epilogue

1. In his creation of a new party, Kadima, at the end of 2005, Sharon explicitly asserted that there would be no more unilateral steps (such as the disengagement from Gaza), though few believed that he would in fact switch to negotiations. Rather, it was rumored—and generally believed—that Sharon planned to continue evacuating settlements from the West Bank.
2. As of this writing, still more changes in the demarcation of the separation barrier were being laid down by the Court (*Ha'aretz*, 19 June 2006).
3. *Ha'aretz*, 22 May 2006.
4. Israel's formulation was recognition of Israel's right to exist (the same formulation previously demanded of the PLO). Notably missing was the demand for recognition as "a Jewish state" stipulated in Israel's fourteen reservations to the Road Map.
5. Iran agreed to provide some funds, although there appeared to be no banks willing to cooperate in getting the funds to the PA; some governments (e.g., Sweden, Russia, and Turkey) agreed to at least meet with representatives of the Hamas government, and the Europeans worked out a plan for the transfer of funds for humanitarian purposes (to health facilities, for example).

6. Palestine Center for Political and Social Research, PSR Poll #19, 16–18 March 2006. A JMCC poll (no.60) mid-September 2006 showed a decline in support for Hamas, bringing the two parties to virtually equal standing in the public.(Press Release, www.jmcc.org.)

7. The popular Fatah leader Marwan Barghouti was among the initiators of the letter, and his status as well as that of the other detainees made it difficult for any Palestinian leadership (inside or outside of prison, inside or outside of the occupied territories) to ignore at the time.

8. Poll conducted by *Ha'aretz*, published 9 June 2006, showing fifty-six percent of Israelis opposed to the convergence plan (presumably including opposition from the left, i.e., those advocating negotiations, as well as from the right, those opposing any withdrawal); the Peace Index of May 2006 found forty-seven percent support for the plan, forty-four percent opposed (*Ha'aretz*, 8 June 2006).

Letters of Mutual Recognition

1. LETTER FROM YASSER ARAFAT TO PRIME MINISTER RABIN:

September 9, 1993

Yitzhak Rabin
Prime Minister of Israel

Mr. Prime Minister,

The signing of the Declaration of Principles marks a new era in the history of the Middle East. In firm conviction thereof, I would like to confirm the following PLO commitments:

The PLO recognizes the right of the State of Israel to exist in peace and security.

The PLO accepts United Nations Security Council Resolutions 242 and 338.

The PLO commits itself to the Middle East peace process, and to a peaceful resolution of the conflict between the two sides and declares that all outstanding issues relating to permanent status will be resolved through negotiations.

The PLO considers that the signing of the Declaration of Principles constitutes a historic event, inaugurating a new epoch of peaceful coexistence, free from violence and all other acts which endanger peace and stability. Accordingly, the PLO renounces the use of terrorism and other acts of violence and will assume responsibility over all PLO elements and personnel in order to assure their compliance, prevent violations and discipline violators.

In view of the promise of a new era and the signing of the Declaration of Principles and based on Palestinian acceptance of Security Council Resolutions 242 and 338, the PLO affirms that those articles of the Palestinian Covenant which deny Israel's right to exist, and the provisions of the Covenant which are inconsistent with the commitments of this letter are now inoperative and no longer valid. Consequently, the PLO undertakes to submit to the Palestinian National Council for formal approval the necessary changes in regard to the Palestinian Covenant.

Sincerely,

Yasser Arafat
Chairman
The Palestine Liberation Organization

2. LETTER FROM YASSER ARAFAT TO NORWEGIAN FOREIGN MINISTER:

September 9, 1993

His Excellency
Johan Jorgen Holst
Foreign Minister of Norway

Dear Minister Holst,

I would like to confirm to you that, upon the signing of the Declaration of Principles, the PLO encourages and calls upon the Palestinian people in the West Bank and Gaza Strip to take part in the steps leading to the normalization of life, rejecting violence and terrorism, contributing to peace and stability and participating actively in shaping reconstruction, economic development and cooperation.

Sincerely,

Yasser Arafat
Chairman
The Palestine Liberation Organization

3. LETTER FROM PRIME MINISTER RABIN TO YASSER ARAFAT:

September 9, 1993

Yasser Arafat
Chairman
The Palestinian Liberation Organization

Mr. Chairman,

In response to your letter of September 9, 1993, I wish to confirm to you that, in light of the PLO commitments included in your letter, the Government of Israel has decided to recognize the PLO as the representative of the Palestinian people and commence negotiations with the PLO within the Middle East peace process.

Sincerely,

Yitzhak Rabin
Prime Minister of Israel

Declaration of Principles on Interim Self-Government Arrangements— September 13, 1993

The Government of the State of Israel and the P.L.O. team (in the Jordanian-Palestinian delegation to the Middle East Peace Conference) (the "Palestinian Delegation"), representing the Palestinian people, agree that it is time to put an end to decades of confrontation and conflict, recognize their mutual legitimate and political rights, and strive to live in peaceful coexistence and mutual dignity and security and achieve a just, lasting and comprehensive peace settlement and historic reconciliation through the agreed political process. Accordingly, the, two sides agree to the following principles:

ARTICLE I
Aim of the Negotiations

The aim of the Israeli-Palestinian negotiations within the current Middle East peace process is, among other things, to establish a Palestinian Interim Self-Government Authority, the elected Council (the "Council"), for the Palestinian people in the West Bank and the Gaza Strip, for a transitional period not exceeding five years, leading to a permanent settlement based on Security Council Resolutions 242 and 338.

It is understood that the interim arrangements are an integral part of the whole peace process and that the negotiations on the permanent status will lead to the implementation of Security Council Resolutions 242 and 338.

ARTICLE II
Framework for the Interim Period

The agreed framework for the interim period is set forth in this Declaration of Principles.

ARTICLE III
Elections

1. In order that the Palestinian people in the West Bank and Gaza Strip may govern themselves according to democratic principles, direct, free and general political elections will be held for the Council under agreed supervision and international observation, while the Palestinian police will ensure public order.
2. An agreement will be concluded on the exact mode and conditions of the elections in accordance with the protocol attached as Annex I, with the goal of holding the elections not later than nine months after the entry into force of this Declaration of Principles.
3. These elections will constitute a significant interim preparatory step toward the realization of the legitimate rights of the Palestinian people and their just requirements.

ARTICLE IV
Jurisdiction

Jurisdiction of the Council will cover West Bank and Gaza Strip territory, except for issues that will be negotiated in the permanent status negotiations. The two sides view the West Bank and the Gaza Strip as a single territorial unit, whose integrity will be preserved during the interim period.

ARTICLE V
Transitional Period and Permanent Status Negotiations

1. The five-year transitional period will begin upon the withdrawal from the Gaza Strip and Jericho area.
2. Permanent status negotiations will commence as soon as possible, but not later than the beginning of the third year of the interim period, between the Government of Israel and the Palestinian people representatives.
3. It is understood that these negotiations shall cover remaining issues, including: Jerusalem, refugees, settlements, security arrangements, borders, relations and cooperation with other neighbors, and other issues of common interest.
4. The two parties agree that the outcome of the permanent status negotiations should not be prejudiced or preempted by agreements reached for the interim period.

ARTICLE VI
Preparatory Transfer of Powers and Responsibilities

1. Upon the entry into force of this Declaration of Principles and the withdrawal from the Gaza Strip and the Jericho area, a transfer of authority from the Israeli military government and its Civil Administration to the authorised Palestinians for this task, as detailed herein, will commence. This transfer of authority will be of a preparatory nature until the inauguration of the Council.
2. Immediately after the entry into force of this Declaration of Principles and the withdrawal from the Gaza Strip and Jericho area, with the view to promoting economic development in the West Bank and Gaza Strip, authority will be transferred to the Palestinians on the following spheres: education and culture, health, social welfare, direct taxation, and tourism. The Palestinian side will commence in building the Palestinian police force, as agreed upon. Pending the inauguration of the Council, the two parties may negotiate the transfer of additional powers and responsibilities, as agreed upon.

ARTICLE VII
Interim Agreement

1. The Israeli and Palestinian delegations will negotiate an agreement on the interim period (the "Interim Agreement")
2. The Interim Agreement shall specify, among other things, the structure of the Council, the number of its members, and the transfer of powers and responsibilities from the Israeli military government and its Civil Administration to the Council. The Interim Agreement shall also specify the Council's executive authority, legislative authority in accordance with Article IX below, and the independent Palestinian judicial organs.
3. The Interim Agreement shall include arrangements, to be implemented upon the inauguration of the Council, for the assumption by the Council of all of the powers and responsibilities transferred previously in accordance with Article VI above.
4. In order to enable the Council to promote economic growth, upon its inauguration, the Council will establish, among other things, a Palestinian Electricity Authority, a Gaza Sea Port Authority, a Palestinian Development Bank, a Palestinian Export Promotion Board, a Palestinian Environmental Authority, a Palestinian Land Authority and a Palestinian Water Administration Authority, and any other Authorities agreed upon, in accordance with the Interim Agreement that will specify their powers and responsibilities.
5. After the inauguration of the Council, the Civil Administration will be dissolved, and the Israeli military government will be withdrawn.

ARTICLE VIII
Public Order and Security

In order to guarantee public order and internal security for the Palestinians of the West Bank and the Gaza Strip, the Council will establish a strong police force, while Israel will continue to carry the responsibility for defending against external threats, as well as the responsibility for overall security of Israelis for the purpose of safeguarding their internal security and public order.

ARTICLE IX
Laws and Military Orders

1. The Council will be empowered to legislate, in accordance with the Interim Agreement, within all authorities transferred to it.
2. Both parties will review jointly laws and military orders presently in force in remaining spheres.

ARTICLE X
Joint Israeli-Palestinian Liaison Committee

In order to provide for a smooth implementation of this Declaration of Principles and any subsequent agreements pertaining to the interim period, upon the entry into force of this Declaration of Principles, a Joint Israeli-Palestinian Liaison Committee will be established in order to deal with issues requiring coordination, other issues of common interest, and disputes.

ARTICLE XI
Israeli-Palestinian Cooperation in Economic Fields

Recognizing the mutual benefit of cooperation in promoting the development of the West Bank, the Gaza Strip and Israel, upon the entry into force of this Declaration of Principles, an Israeli-Palestinian Economic Cooperation Committee will be established in order to develop and implement in a cooperative manner the programs identified in the protocols attached as Annex III and Annex IV.

ARTICLE XII
Liaison and Cooperation with Jordan and Egypt

The two parties will invite the Governments of Jordan and Egypt to participate in establishing further liaison and cooperation arrangements between the Government of Israel and the Palestinian representatives, on the one hand, and the Governments of Jordan and Egypt, on the other hand, to promote cooperation between them. These arrangements will include the constitution of a Continuing Committee that will decide by agreement on the modalities of admission of persons displaced from the West Bank and Gaza Strip in 1967, together with necessary measures to prevent disruption and disorder. Other matters of common concern will be dealt with by this Committee.

ARTICLE XIII
Redeployment of Israeli Forces

1. After the entry into force of this Declaration of Principles, and not later than the eve of elections for the Council, a redeployment of Israeli military forces in the West Bank and the Gaza Strip will take place, in addition to withdrawal of Israeli forces carried out in accordance with Article XIV.
2. In redeploying its military forces, Israel will be guided by the principle that its military forces should be redeployed outside populated areas.
3. Further redeployments to specified locations will be gradually implemented commensurate with the assumption of responsibility for public order and internal security by the Palestinian police force pursuant to Article VIII above.

ARTICLE XIV
Israeli Withdrawal from the Gaza Strip and Jericho Area

Israel will withdraw from the Gaza Strip and Jericho area, as detailed in the protocol attached as Annex II.

ARTICLE XV
Resolution of Disputes

1. Disputes arising out of the application or interpretation of this Declaration of Principles. or any subsequent agreements pertaining to the interim period, shall be resolved by negotiations through the Joint Liaison Committee to be established pursuant to Article X above.
2. Disputes which cannot be settled by negotiations may be resolved by a mechanism of conciliation to be agreed upon by the parties.

3. The parties may agree to submit to arbitration disputes relating to the interim period, which cannot be settled through conciliation. To this end, upon the agreement of both parties, the parties will establish an Arbitration Committee.

ARTICLE XVI
Israeli-Palestinian Cooperation Concerning Regional Programs

Both parties view the multilateral working groups as an appropriate instrument for promoting a "Marshall Plan", the regional programs and other programs, including special programs for the West Bank and Gaza Strip, as indicated in the protocol attached as Annex IV.

ARTICLE XVII
Miscellaneous Provisions

1. This Declaration of Principles will enter into force one month after its signing.
2. All protocols annexed to this Declaration of Principles and Agreed Minutes pertaining thereto shall be regarded as an integral part hereof.

Done at Washington, D.C., this thirteenth day of September, 1993.

For the Government of Israel
For the P.L.O.

Witnessed By:

The United States of America
The Russian Federation

ANNEX I
Protocol on the Mode and Conditions of Elections

1. Palestinians of Jerusalem who live there will have the right to participate in the election process, according to an agreement between the two sides.

2. In addition, the election agreement should cover, among other things, the following issues:
   1. the system of elections;
   2. the mode of the agreed supervision and international observation and their personal composition; and
   3. rules and regulations regarding election campaign, including agreed arrangements for the organizing of mass media, and the possibility of licensing a broadcasting and TV station.

3. The future status of displaced Palestinians who were registered on 4th June 1967 will not be prejudiced because they are unable to participate in the election process due to practical reasons.

ANNEX II
Protocol on Withdrawal of Israeli Forces from the Gaza Strip and Jericho Area

1. The two sides will conclude and sign within two months from the date of entry into force of this Declaration of Principles, an agreement on the withdrawal of Israeli military forces from the Gaza Strip and Jericho area. This agreement will include comprehensive arrangements to apply in the Gaza Strip and the Jericho area subsequent to the Israeli withdrawal.

2. Israel will implement an accelerated and scheduled withdrawal of Israeli military forces from the Gaza Strip and Jericho area, beginning immediately with the signing of the agreement on the Gaza Strip and Jericho area and to be completed within a period not exceeding four months after the signing of this agreement.

3. The above agreement will include, among other things:
   1. Arrangements for a smooth and peaceful transfer of authority from

the Israeli military government and its Civil Administration to the Palestinian representatives.

2. Structure, powers and responsibilities of the Palestinian authority in these areas, except: external security, settlements, Israelis, foreign relations, and other mutually agreed matters.

3. Arrangements for the assumption of internal security and public order by the Palestinian police force consisting of police officers recruited locally and from abroad holding Jordanian passports and Palestinian documents issued by Egypt. Those who will participate in the Palestinian police force coming from abroad should be trained as police and police officers.

4. A temporary international or foreign presence, as agreed upon.

5. Establishment of a joint Palestinian-Israeli Coordination and Coordination Committee for mutual security purposes.

6. An economic development and stabilization program, including the establishment of an Emergency Fund, to encourage foreign investment, and financial and economic support. Both sides will coordinate and cooperate jointly and unilaterally with regional and international parties to support these aims.

7. Arrangements for a safe passage for persons and transportation between the Gaza Strip and Jericho area.

4. The above agreement will include arrangements for coordination between both parties regarding passages:

   1. Gaza – Egypt; and
   2. Jericho – Jordan.

5. The offices responsible for carrying out the powers and responsibilities of the Palestinian authority under this Annex II and Article VI of the Declaration of Principles will be located in the Gaza Strip and in the Jericho area pending the inauguration of the Council.

6. Other than these agreed arrangements, the status of the Gaza Strip and Jericho area will continue to be an integral part of the West Bank and Gaza Strip, and will not be changed in the interim period.

ANNEX III

Protocol on Israeli-Palestinian Cooperation in Economic and Development Programs

The two sides agree to establish an Israeli-Palestinian continuing Committee for Economic Cooperation, focusing, among other things, on the following:

1. Cooperation in the field of water, including a Water Development Program prepared by experts from both sides, which will also specify the mode of cooperation in the management of water resources in the West Bank and Gaza Strip, and will include proposals for studies and plans on water rights of each party, as well as on the equitable utilization of joint water resources for implementation in and beyond the interim period.

2. Cooperation in the field of electricity, including an Electricity Development Program, which will also specify the mode of cooperation for the production, maintenance, purchase and sale of electricity resources.

3. Cooperation in the field of energy, including an Energy Development Program, which will provide for the exploitation of oil and gas for industrial purposes, particularly in the Gaza Strip and in the Negev, and will encourage further joint exploitation of other energy resources. This Program may also provide for the construction of a Petrochemical industrial complex in the Gaza Strip and the construction of oil and gas pipelines.

4. Cooperation in the field of finance, including a Financial Development and Action Program for the encouragement of international investment in the West Bank and the Gaza Strip, and in Israel, as well as the establishment of a Palestinian Development Bank.

5. Cooperation in the field of transport and communications, including a Program, which will define guidelines for the establishment of a Gaza Sea Port Area, and will provide for the establishing of transport and communications lines to and from the West Bank and the Gaza Strip to Israel and to other countries. In addition, this Program will provide for carrying out the necessary construction of roads, railways, communications lines, etc.

6. Cooperation in the field of trade, including studies, and Trade Promotion Programs, which will encourage local, regional and inter-regional trade, as well as a feasibility study of creating free trade zones in the Gaza Strip and in Israel, mutual access to these zones, and cooperation in other areas related to trade and commerce.

7. Cooperation in the field of industry, including Industrial Development Programs, which will provide for the establishment of joint Israeli-Palestinian Industrial Research and Development Centers, will promote Palestinian-Israeli joint ventures, and provide guidelines for cooperation in the textile, food, pharmaceutical, electronics, diamonds, computer and science-based industries.

8. A program for cooperation in, and regulation of, labor relations and cooperation in social welfare issues.

9. A Human Resources Development and Cooperation Plan, providing for joint Israeli-Palestinian workshops and seminars, and for the establishment of joint vocational training centers, research institutes and data banks.

10. An Environmental Protection Plan, providing for joint and/or coordinated measures in this sphere.

11. A program for developing coordination and cooperation in the field of communication and media.

12. Any other programs of mutual interest.

ANNEX IV
Protocol on Israeli-Palestinian Cooperation Concerning Regional Development Programs

1. The two sides will cooperate in the context of the multilateral peace efforts in promoting a Development Program for the region, including the West Bank and the Gaza Strip, to be initiated by the G-7. The parties will request the G-7 to seek the participation in this program of other interested states, such as members of the Organisation for Economic Cooperation and Development, regional Arab states and institutions, as well as members of the private sector.

2. The Development Program will consist of two elements:
   1. an Economic Development Program for the West Bank and the Gaza Strip.
   2. a Regional Economic Development Program.
      1. The Economic Development Program for the West Bank and the Gaza strip will consist of the following elements:
         1. A Social Rehabilitation Program, including a Housing and Construction Program.
         2. A Small and Medium Business Development Plan.
         3. An Infrastructure Development Program (water, electricity, transportation and communications, etc.)
         4. A Human Resources Plan.
         5. Other programs.
      2. The Regional Economic Development Program may consist of the following elements:
         1. The establishment of a Middle East Development Fund, as a first step, and a Middle East Development Bank, as a second step.
         2. The development of a joint Israeli-Palestinian-Jordanian Plan for coordinated exploitation of the Dead Sea area.
         3. The Mediterranean Sea (Gaza) – Dead Sea Canal.
         4. Regional Desalinization and other water development projects.
         5. A regional plan for agricultural development, including a coordinated regional effort for the prevention of desertification.
         6. Interconnection of electricity grids.
         7. Regional cooperation for the transfer, distribution and industrial exploitation of gas, oil and other energy resources.
         8. A Regional Tourism, Transportation and Telecommunications Development Plan.
         9. Regional cooperation in other spheres.
   3. The two sides will encourage the multilateral working groups, and will coordinate towards their success. The two parties will encourage intersessional activities, as well as pre-feasibility and feasibility studies, within the various multilateral working groups.

AGREED MINUTES TO THE DECLARATION OF PRINCIPLES ON INTERIM SELF-GOVERNMENT ARRANGEMENTS

A. GENERAL UNDERSTANDINGS AND AGREEMENTS

Any powers and responsibilities transferred to the Palestinians pursuant to the Declaration of Principles prior to the inauguration of the Council will be subject to the same principles pertaining to Article IV, as set out in these Agreed Minutes below.

B. SPECIFIC UNDERSTANDINGS AND AGREEMENTS

Article IV

It is understood that:

1. Jurisdiction of the Council will cover West Bank and Gaza Strip territory, except for issues that will be negotiated in the permanent status negotiations: Jerusalem, settlements, military locations, and Israelis.
2. The Council's jurisdiction will apply with regard to the agreed powers, responsibilities, spheres and authorities transferred to it.

Article VI (2)

It is agreed that the transfer of authority will be as follows:

1. The Palestinian side will inform the Israeli side of the names of the authorised Palestinians who will assume the powers, authorities and responsibilities that will be transferred to the Palestinians according to the Declaration of Principles in the following fields: education and culture, health, social welfare, direct taxation, tourism, and any other authorities agreed upon.
2. It is understood that the rights and obligations of these offices will not be affected.
3. Each of the spheres described above will continue to enjoy existing budgetary allocations in accordance with arrangements to be mutually agreed upon. These arrangements also will provide for the necessary

adjustments required in order to take into account the taxes collected by the direct taxation office.

4. Upon the execution of the Declaration of Principles, the Israeli and Palestinian delegations will immediately commence negotiations on a detailed plan for the transfer of authority on the above offices in accordance with the above understandings.

Article VII (2)

The Interim Agreement will also include arrangements for coordination and cooperation.

Article VII (5)

The withdrawal of the military government will not prevent Israel from exercising the powers and responsibilities not transferred to the Council.

Article VIII

It is understood that the Interim Agreement will include arrangements for cooperation and coordination between the two parties in this regard. It is also agreed that the transfer of powers and responsibilities to the Palestinian police will be accomplished in a phased manner, as agreed in the Interim Agreement.

Article X

It is agreed that, upon the entry into force of the Declaration of Principles, the Israeli and Palestinian delegations will exchange the names of the individuals designated by them as members of the Joint Israeli-Palestinian Liaison Committee.

It is further agreed that each side will have an equal number of members in the Joint Committee. The Joint Committee will reach decisions by agreement. The Joint Committee may add other technicians and experts, as necessary.

The Joint Committee will decide on the frequency and place or places of its meetings.

Annex II

It is understood that, subsequent to the Israeli withdrawal, Israel will continue to be responsible for external security, and for internal security and public order of settlements and Israelis. Israeli military forces and civilians may continue to use roads freely within the Gaza Strip and the Jericho area.

Done at Washington, D.C., this thirteenth day of September, 1993.

For the Government of Israel
For the P.L.O.

Witnessed By:
The United States of America
The Russian Federation

Arab Peace Initiative—Beirut Summit

The Arab Peace Initiative
The Council of the League of Arab States at the Summit Level, at its 14th Ordinary Session,

- Reaffirming the resolution taken in June 1996 at the Cairo Extra-Ordinary Arab Summit that a just and comprehensive peace in the Middle East is the strategic option of the Arab Countries, to be achieved in accordance with International Legality, and which would require a comparable commitment on the part of the Israeli Government.
- Having listened to the statement made by His Royal Highness Prince Abdullah bin Abdul Aziz, the Crown Prince of the Kingdom of Saudi Arabia in which his Highness presented his Initiative, calling for full Israeli withdrawal from all the Arab territories occupied since June 1967, in implementation of Security Council Resolutions 242 and 338, reaffirmed by the Madrid Conference of 1991 and the land for peace principle, and Israel's acceptance of an independent Palestinian state, with East Jerusalem as its capital, in return for the establishment of normal relations in the context of a comprehensive peace with Israel.

185

- Emanating from the conviction of the Arab countries that a military solution to the conflict will not achieve peace or provide security for the parties, the council:
  1. Requests Israel to reconsider its policies and declare that a just peace is its strategic option as well.
  2. Further calls upon Israel to affirm:
     a. Full Israeli withdrawal from all the territories occupied since 1967, including the Syrian Golan Heights to the lines of June 4, 1967 as well as the remaining occupied Lebanese territories in the south of Lebanon.
     b. Achievement of a just solution to the Palestinian Refugee problem to be agreed upon in accordance with UN General Assembly Resolution 194.
     c. The acceptance of the establishment of a Sovereign Independent Palestinian State on the Palestinian territories occupied since the 4th of June 1967 in the West Bank and Gaza strip, with East Jerusalem as its capital.
  3. Consequently, the Arab Countries affirm the following:
     a. Consider the Arab-Israeli conflict ended, and enter into a peace agreement with Israel, and provide security for all the states of the region.
     b. Establish normal relations with Israel in the context of this comprehensive peace.
  4. Assures the rejection of all forms of Palestinian patriation which conflict with the special circumstances of the Arab host countries.
  5. Calls upon the Government of Israel and all Israelis to accept this initiative in order to safeguard the prospects for peace and stop the further shedding of blood, enabling the Arab Countries and Israel to live in peace and good neighborliness and provide future generations with security, stability, and prosperity.
  6. Invites the International Community and all countries and Organizations to support this initiative.
  7. Requests the Chairman of the Summit to form a special committee composed of some of its concerned member states and the Secretary

General of the League of Arab States to pursue the necessary contacts to gain support for this initiative at all levels, particularly from the United Nations, the Security Council, the United States of America, the Russian Federation, the Muslim States, and the European Union.

[BEIRUT, March 28 (AFP) – The official translation of the Saudi-proposed Arab peace initiative adopted at the annual Arab summit in Beirut, as published on the Arab League internet site.]

Road Map

The full text of a roadmap to peace in the Middle East, presented to Palestinian and Israeli leaders by Quartet mediators—the United Nations, European Union, United States and Russia.

A performance-based roadmap to a permanent two-state solution to the Israeli-Palestinian conflict.

The following is a performance-based and goal-driven roadmap, with clear phases, timelines, target dates, and benchmarks aiming at progress through reciprocal steps by the two parties in the political, security, economic, humanitarian, and institution-building fields, under the auspices of the Quartet.

The destination is a final and comprehensive settlement of the Israeli-Palestinian conflict by 2005, as presented in President Bush's speech of 24 June, and welcomed by the EU, Russia and the UN in the 16 July and 17 September Quartet Ministerial statements.

A two-state solution to the Israeli-Palestinian conflict will only be achieved through an end to violence and terrorism, when the Palestinian people have a leadership acting decisively against terror and willing and able to build a practicing democracy based on tolerance and liberty, and through Israel's readiness to do what is necessary for a democratic Palestinian State to be established, and a clear, unambiguous acceptance by both parties of the goal of a negotiated settlement as described below.

The Quartet will assist and facilitate implementation of the plan, starting in Phase I, including direct discussions between the parties as required.

The plan establishes a realistic timeline for implementation.

However, as a performance-based plan, progress will require and depend upon the good faith efforts of the parties, and their compliance with each of the obligations outlined below.

Should the parties perform their obligations rapidly, progress within and through the phases may come sooner than indicated in the plan.

Non-compliance with obligations will impede progress.

A settlement, negotiated between the parties, will result in the emergence of an independent, democratic, and viable living side by side in peace and security with Israel and its other neighbours.

The settlement will resolve the Israel-Palestinian conflict, and end the occupation that began in 1967, based on the foundations of the Madrid Conference, the principle of land for peace, UNSCRs 242, 338 and 1397, agreements previously reached by the parties, and the initiative of Saudi Crown Prince Abdullah—endorsed by the Beirut Arab League Summit—calling for acceptance of Israel as a neighbour living in peace and security, in the context of a comprehensive settlement.

This initiative is a vital element of international efforts to promote a comprehensive peace on all tracks, including the Syrian-Israeli and Lebanese-Israeli tracks.

The Quartet will meet regularly at senior levels to evaluate the parties' performance on implementation of the plan. In each phase, the parties are expected to perform their obligations in parallel, unless otherwise indicated.

Phase I: Ending terror and violence, normalising Palestinian life, and building Palestinian institutions (present to May 2003)

In Phase I, the Palestinians immediately undertake an unconditional cessation of violence according to the steps outlined below; such action should be accompanied by supportive measures undertaken by Israel.

Palestinians and Israelis resume security co-operation based on the Tenet work plan to end violence, terrorism, and incitement through restructured and effective Palestinian security services.

Palestinians undertake comprehensive political reform in preparation for statehood, including drafting a Palestinian constitution, and free, fair and open elections upon the basis of those measures.

Israel takes all necessary steps to help normalise Palestinian life.

Israel withdraws from Palestinian areas occupied from September 28, 2000 and the two sides restore the status quo that existed at that time, as security performance and co-operation progress.

Israel also freezes all settlement activity, consistent with the Mitchell report.

At the outset of Phase I:
- Palestinian leadership issues unequivocal statement reiterating Israel's right to exist in peace and security and calling for an immediate and unconditional ceasefire to end armed activity and all acts of violence against Israelis anywhere. All official Palestinian institutions end incitement against Israel.
- Israeli leadership issues unequivocal statement affirming its commitment to the two-state vision of an independent, viable, sovereign Palestinian State living in peace and security alongside Israel, as expressed by President Bush, and calling for an immediate end to violence against Palestinians everywhere. All official Israeli institutions end incitement against Palestinians.

Security
- Palestinians declare an unequivocal end to violence and terrorism and undertake visible efforts on the ground to arrest, disrupt, and restrain individuals and groups conducting and planning violent attacks on Israelis anywhere.
- Rebuilt and refocused Palestinian Authority security apparatus begins sustained, targeted, and effective operations aimed at confronting all those

engaged in terror and dismantlement of terrorist capabilities and infra-structure. This includes commencing confiscation of illegal weapons and consolidation of security authority, free of association with terror and corruption.

- GOI takes no actions undermining trust, including deportations, attacks on civilians; confiscation and/or demolition of Palestinian homes and prop-erty, as a punitive measure or to facilitate Israeli construction; destruction of Palestinian institutions and infrastructure; and other measures specified in the Tenet work plan.
- Relying on existing mechanisms and on-the-ground resources, Quartet representatives begin informal monitoring and consult with the parties on establishment of a formal monitoring mechanism and its implementation.
- Implementation, as previously agreed, of US rebuilding, training and re-sumed security co-operation plan in collaboration with outside oversight board (US-Egypt-Jordan). Quartet support for efforts to achieve a lasting, comprehensive ceasefire.
  - All Palestinian security organizations are consolidated into three services reporting to an empowered Interior Minister.
  - Restructured/retrained Palestinian security forces and IDF counterparts progressively resume security co-operation and other undertakings in implementation of the Tenet work plan, including regular senior-level meetings, with the participation of US security officials.
- Arab states cut off public and private funding and all other forms of sup-port for groups supporting and engaging in violence and terror.
- All donors providing budgetary support for the Palestinians channel these funds through the Palestinian Ministry of Finance's Single Treasury Ac-count.
- As comprehensive security performance moves forward, IDF withdraws progressively from areas occupied since 28 September 2000 and the two sides restore the status quo that existed prior to 28 September 2000. Pales-tinian security forces redeploy to areas vacated by IDF.

Palestinian institution-building
- Immediate action on credible process to produce draft constitution for Palestinian statehood. As rapidly as possible, constitutional committee

circulates draft Palestinian constitution, based on strong parliamentary democracy and cabinet with empowered prime minister, for public comment/debate. Constitutional committee proposes draft document for submission after elections for approval by appropriate Palestinian institutions.

- Appointment of interim prime minister or cabinet with empowered executive authority/decision-making body.
- GOI fully facilitates travel of Palestinian officials for PLC and cabinet sessions, internationally supervised security retraining, electoral and other reform activity, and other supportive measures related to the reform efforts.
- Continued appointment of Palestinian ministers empowered to undertake fundamental reform. Completion of further steps to achieve genuine separation of powers, including any necessary Palestinian legal reforms for this purpose.
- Establishment of independent Palestinian election commission. PLC reviews and revises election law.
- Palestinian performance on judicial, administrative, and economic benchmarks, as established by the International Task Force on Palestinian Reform.
- As early as possible, and based upon the above measures and in the context of open debate and transparent candidate selection/electoral campaign based on a free, multi-party process, Palestinians hold free, open, and fair elections.
- GOI facilitates Task Force election assistance, registration of voters, movement of candidates and voting officials. Support for NGOs involved in the election process.
- GOI reopens Palestinian Chamber of Commerce and other closed Palestinian institutions in East Jerusalem based on a commitment that these institutions operate strictly in accordance with prior agreements between the parties.

Humanitarian response

- Israel takes measures to improve the humanitarian situation. Israel and Palestinians implement in full all recommendations of the Bertini report to improve humanitarian conditions, lifting curfews and easing restrictions on movement of persons and goods, and allowing full, safe, and unfettered access of international and humanitarian personnel.

- AHLC reviews the humanitarian situation and prospects for economic development in the West Bank and Gaza and launches a major donor assistance effort, including to the reform effort.
- GOI and PA continue revenue clearance process and transfer of funds, including arrears, in accordance with agreed, transparent monitoring mechanism.

Civil society

- Continued donor support, including increased funding through PVOs/NGOs, for people to people programs, private sector development and civil society initiatives.

Settlements

- GOI immediately dismantles settlement outposts erected since March 2001.
- Consistent with the Mitchell Report, GOI freezes all settlement activity (including natural growth of settlements).

Phase II: Transition (June 2003–December 2003)

In the second phase, efforts are focused on the option of creating an independent Palestinian state with provisional borders and attributes of sovereignty, based on the new constitution, as a way station to a permanent status settlement.

As has been noted, this goal can be achieved when the Palestinian people have a leadership acting decisively against terror, willing and able to build a practicing democracy based on tolerance and liberty.

With such a leadership, reformed civil institutions and security structures, the Palestinians will have the active support of the Quartet and the broader international community in establishing an independent, viable, state.

Progress into Phase II will be based upon the consensus judgment of the Quartet of whether conditions are appropriate to proceed, taking into account performance of both parties.

Furthering and sustaining efforts to normalise Palestinian lives and build Palestinian institutions, Phase II starts after Palestinian elections and ends with possible creation of an independent Palestinian state with provisional borders in 2003.

Its primary goals are continued comprehensive security performance and effective security co-operation, continued normalisation of Palestinian life and institution-building, further building on and sustaining of the goals outlined in Phase I, ratification of a democratic Palestinian constitution, formal establishment of office of prime minister, consolidation of political reform, and the creation of a Palestinian state with provisional borders.

- International conference: Convened by the Quartet, in consultation with the parties, immediately after the successful conclusion of Palestinian elections, to support Palestinian economic recovery and launch a process, leading to establishment of an independent Palestinian state with provisional borders.
  - Such a meeting would be inclusive, based on the goal of a comprehensive Middle East peace (including between Israel and Syria, and Israel and Lebanon), and based on the principles described in the preamble to this document.
  - Arab states restore pre-intifada links to Israel (trade offices, etc.).
  - Revival of multilateral engagement on issues including regional water resources, environment, economic development, refugees, and arms control issues.
- New constitution for democratic, independent Palestinian state is finalised and approved by appropriate Palestinian institutions. Further elections, if required, should follow approval of the new constitution.
- Empowered reform cabinet with office of prime minister formally established, consistent with draft constitution.
- Continued comprehensive security performance, including effective security cooperation on the bases laid out in Phase I.
- Creation of an independent Palestinian state with provisional borders through a process of Israeli-Palestinian engagement, launched by the international conference. As part of this process, implementation of prior agreements, to enhance maximum territorial contiguity, including further action on settlements in conjunction with establishment of a Palestinian state with provisional borders.

- Enhanced international role in monitoring transition, with the active, sustained, and operational support of the Quartet.
- Quartet members promote international recognition of Palestinian state, including possible UN membership.

Phase III: Permanent status agreement and end of the Israeli-Palestinian conflict (2004–2005)

Progress into Phase III, based on consensus judgment of Quartet, and taking into account actions of both parties and Quartet monitoring.

Phase III objectives are consolidation of reform and stabilisation of Palestinian institutions, sustained, effective Palestinian security performance, and Israeli-Palestinian negotiations aimed at a permanent status agreement in 2005.

- Second international conference: Convened by Quartet, in consultation with the parties, at beginning of 2004 to endorse agreement reached on an independent Palestinian state with provisional borders and formally to launch a process with the active, sustained, and operational support of the Quartet, leading to a final, permanent status resolution in 2005, including on borders, Jerusalem, refugees, settlements; and, to support progress toward a comprehensive Middle East settlement between Israel and Lebanon and Israel and Syria, to be achieved as soon as possible.
- Continued comprehensive, effective progress on the reform agenda laid out by the Task Force in preparation for final status agreement.
- Continued sustained and effective security performance, and sustained, effective security cooperation on the bases laid out in Phase I.
- International efforts to facilitate reform and stabilise Palestinian institutions and the Palestinian economy, in preparation for final status agreement.
- Parties reach final and comprehensive permanent status agreement that ends the Israeli-Palestinian conflict in 2005, through a settlement negotiated between the parties based on UNSCR 242, 338, and 1397, that ends the occupation that began in 1967, and includes an agreed, just, fair, and realistic solution to the refugee issue, and a negotiated resolution on the status of Jerusalem that takes into account the political and religious concerns of both sides, and protects the religious interests of Jews,

Christians, and Muslims worldwide, and fulfils the vision of two states, Israel and sovereign, independent, democratic and viable Palestine, living side-by-side in peace and security.

- Arab state acceptance of full normal relations with Israel and security for all the states of the region in the context of a comprehensive Arab-Israeli peace.

The Geneva Accord— A Model Agreement

Article 7 – Refugees

1. **Significance of the Refugee Problem**
    i.   The Parties recognize that, in the context of two independent states, Palestine and Israel, living side by side in peace, an agreed resolution of the refugee problem is necessary for achieving a just, comprehensive and lasting peace between them.
    ii. Such a resolution will also be central to stability building and development in the region.

2. **UNGAR 194, UNSC Resolution 242, and the Arab Peace Initiative**
    i.   The Parties recognize that UNGAR 194, UNSC Resolution 242, and the Arab Peace Initiative (Article 2.ii.) concerning the rights of the Palestinian refugees represent the basis for resolving the refugee issue, and agree that these rights are fulfilled according to Article 7 of this Agreement.

3. **Compensation**

   i.   Refugees shall be entitled to compensation for their refugeehood and for loss of property. This shall not prejudice or be prejudiced by the refugee's permanent place of residence.

   ii.   The Parties recognize the right of states that have hosted Palestinian refugees to remuneration.

4. **Choice of Permanent Place of Residence (PPR)**

The solution to the PPR aspect of the refugee problem shall entail an act of informed choice on the part of the refugee to be exercised in accordance with the options and modalities set forth in this agreement. PPR options from which the refugees may choose shall be as follows;

   i.   The state of Palestine, in accordance with clause a below.

   ii.   Areas in Israel being transferred to Palestine in the land swap, following assumption of Palestinian sovereignty, in accordance with clause a below.

   iii. Third Countries, in accordance with clause b below.

   iv. The state of Israel, in accordance with clause c below.

   v.   Present Host countries, in accordance with clause d below.

       a.   PPR options i and ii shall be the right of all Palestinian refugees and shall be in accordance with the laws of the State of Palestine.

       b.   Option iii shall be at the sovereign discretion of third countries and shall be in accordance with numbers that each third country will submit to the International Commission. These numbers shall represent the total number of Palestinian refugees that each third country shall accept.

       c.   Option iv shall be at the sovereign discretion of Israel and will be in accordance with a number that Israel will submit to the International Commission. This number shall represent the total number of Palestinian refugees that Israel shall accept. As a basis, Israel will consider the average of the total numbers submitted by the different third countries to the International Commission.

    d.   Option v shall be in accordance with the sovereign discretion of present host countries. Where exercised this shall be in the context of prompt and extensive development and rehabilitation programs for the refugee communities

Priority in all the above shall be accorded to the Palestinian refugee population in Lebanon.

5. **Free and Informed Choice**

The process by which Palestinian refugees shall express their PPR choice shall be on the basis of a free and informed decision. The Parties themselves are committed and will encourage third parties to facilitate the refugees' free choice in expressing their preferences, and to countering any attempts at interference or organized pressure on the process of choice. This will not prejudice the recognition of Palestine as the realization of Palestinian self-determination and statehood.

6. **End of Refugee Status**

Palestinian refugee status shall be terminated upon the realization of an individual refugee's permanent place of residence (PPR) as determined by the International Commission.

7. **End of Claims**

This agreement provides for the permanent and complete resolution of the Palestinian refugee problem. No claims may be raised except for those related to the implementation of this agreement.

8. **International Role**

The Parties call upon the international community to participate fully in the comprehensive resolution of the refugee problem in accordance with this Agreement, including, inter alia, the establishment of an International Commission and an International Fund.

9. **Property Compensation**

    i.   Refugees shall be compensated for the loss of property resulting from their displacement.

    ii.   The aggregate sum of property compensation shall be calculated as follows:

        a.   The Parties shall request the International Commission to appoint a Panel of Experts to estimate the value of Palestinians' property at the time of displacement.

        b.   The Panel of Experts shall base its assessment on the UNCCP records, the records of the Custodian for Absentee Property, and any other records it deems relevant. The Parties shall make these records available to the Panel.

        c.   The Parties shall appoint experts to advise and assist the Panel in its work.

        d.   Within 6 months, the Panel shall submit its estimates to the Parties.

        e.   The Parties shall agree on an economic multiplier, to be applied to the estimates, to reach a fair aggregate value of the property.

    iii.   The aggregate value agreed to by the Parties shall constitute the Israeli "lump sum" contribution to the International Fund. No other financial claims arising from the Palestinian refugee problem may be raised against Israel.

    iv.   Israel's contribution shall be made in installments in accordance with Schedule X.

    v.   The value of the Israeli fixed assets that shall remain intact in former settlements and transferred to the state of Palestine will be deducted from Israel's contribution to the International Fund. An estimation of this value shall be made by the International Fund, taking into account assessment of damage caused by the settlements.

10. Compensation for Refugeehood

    i.   A "Refugeehood Fund" shall be established in recognition of each individual's refugeehood. The Fund, to which Israel shall be a contributing party, shall be overseen by the International Commission. The structure and financing of the Fund is set forth in Annex X.

Hold ID... ABU   3137
09/04/09

LAW Hold Slip
The much too promi

ii.   Funds will be disbursed to refugee communities in the former areas
      of UNRWA operation, and will be at their disposal for communal
      development and commemoration of the refugee experience. Appro-
      priate mechanisms will be devised by the International Commission
      whereby the beneficiary refugee communities are empowered to
      determine and administer the use of this Fund.

11. **The International Commission (Commission)**
  i.   Mandate and Composition
      a.   An International Commission shall be established and shall
           have full and exclusive responsibility for implementing all
           aspects of this Agreement pertaining to refugees.
      b.   In addition to themselves, the Parties call upon the United
           Nations, the United States, UNRWA, the Arab host countries,
           the EU, Switzerland, Canada, Norway, Japan, the World Bank,
           the Russian Federation, and others to be the members of the
           Commission.
      c.   The Commission shall:
           1.   Oversee and manage the process whereby the status and
                PPR of Palestinian refugees is determined and realized.
           2.   Oversee and manage, in close cooperation with the host
                states, the rehabilitation and development programs.
           3.   Raise and disburse funds as appropriate.
      d.   The Parties shall make available to the Commission all relevant
           documentary records and archival materials in their possession
           that it deems necessary for the functioning of the Commission
           and its organs. The Commission may request such materials
           from all other relevant parties and bodies, including, inter alia,
           UNCCP and UNRWA.
  ii. Structure
      a.   The Commission shall be governed by an Executive Board
           (Board) composed of representatives of its members.
      b.   The Board shall be the highest authority in the Commission
           and shall make the relevant policy decisions in accordance with
           this Agreement.

      c.   The Board shall draw up the procedures governing the work of the Commission in accordance with this Agreement.

      d.   The Board shall oversee the conduct of the various Committees of the Commission. The said Committees shall periodically report to the Board in accordance with procedures set forth thereby.

      e.   The Board shall create a Secretariat and appoint a Chair thereof. The Chair and the Secretariat shall conduct the day-to-day operation of the Commission.

iii.   Specific Committees

      a.   The Commission shall establish the Technical Committees specified below.

      b.   Unless otherwise specified in this Agreement, the Board shall determine the structure and procedures of the Committees.

      c.   The Parties may make submissions to the Committees as deemed necessary.

      d.   The Committees shall establish mechanisms for resolution of disputes arising from the interpretation or implementation of the provisions of this Agreement relating to refugees.

      e.   The Committees shall function in accordance with this Agreement, and shall render binding decisions accordingly.

      f.   Refugees shall have the right to appeal decisions affecting them according to mechanisms established by this Agreement and detailed in Annex X.

iv.   Status-determination Committee

      a.   The Status-determination Committee shall be responsible for verifying refugee status.

      b.   UNRWA registration shall be considered as rebuttable presumption (prima facie proof) of refugee status.

v.   Compensation Committee

      a.   The Compensation Committee shall be responsible for administering the implementation of the compensation provisions.

      b.   The Committee shall disburse compensation for individual property pursuant to the following modalities:

1. Either a fixed per capita award for property claims below a specified value. This will require the claimant to only prove title, and shall be processed according to a fast-track procedure, or

2. A claims-based award for property claims exceeding a specified value for immovables and other assets. This will require the claimant to prove both title and the value of the losses.

c. Annex X shall elaborate the details of the above including, but not limited to, evidentiary issues and the use of UNCCP, "Custodian for Absentees' Property", and UNRWA records, along with any other relevant records.

vi. Host State Remuneration Committee:
There shall be remuneration for host states.

vii. Permanent Place of Residence Committee (PPR Committee)
The PPR Committee shall,

a. Develop with all the relevant parties detailed programs regarding the implementation of the PPR options pursuant to Article 7/4 above.

b. Assist the applicants in making an informed choice regarding PPR options.

c. Receive applications from refugees regarding PPR. The applicants must indicate a number of preferences in accordance with article 7/4 above. The applications shall be received no later than two years after the start of the International Commission's operations. Refugees who do not submit such applications within the two-year period shall lose their refugee status.

d. Determine, in accordance with sub-Article (a) above, the PPR of the applicants, taking into account individual preferences and maintenance of family unity. Applicants who do not avail themselves of the Committee's PPR determination shall lose their refugee status.

e. Provide the applicants with the appropriate technical and legal assistance.

  f. The PPR of Palestinian refugees shall be realized within 5 years of the start of the International Commission's operations.

 viii. Refugeehood Fund Committee

  The Refugeehood Fund Committee shall implement Article 7/10 as detailed in Annex X.

 ix. Rehabilitation and Development Committee

  In accordance with the aims of this Agreement and noting the above PPR programs, the Rehabilitation and Development Committee shall work closely with Palestine, Host Countries and other relevant third countries and parties in pursuing the goal of refugee rehabilitation and community development. This shall include devising programs and plans to provide the former refugees with opportunities for personal and communal development, housing, education, healthcare, re-training and other needs. This shall be integrated in the general development plans for the region.

12. The International Fund

 i. An International Fund (the Fund) shall be established to receive contributions outlined in this Article and additional contributions from the international community. The Fund shall disburse monies to the Commission to enable it to carry out its functions. The Fund shall audit the Commission's work.

 ii. The structure, composition and operation of the Fund are set forth in Annex X.

13. UNRWA

 i. UNRWA should be phased out in each country in which it operates, based on the end of refugee status in that country.

 ii. UNRWA should cease to exist five years after the start of the Commission's operations. The Commission shall draw up a plan for the phasing out of UNRWA and shall facilitate the transfer of UNRWA functions to host states.

14. Reconciliation Programs

 i. The Parties will encourage and promote the development of cooperation between their relevant institutions and civil societies in creating forums for exchanging historical narratives and enhancing mutual understanding regarding the past.

ii.   The Parties shall encourage and facilitate exchanges in order to disseminate a richer appreciation of these respective narratives, in the fields of formal and informal education, by providing conditions for direct contacts between schools, educational institutions and civil society.

iii. The Parties may consider cross-community cultural programs in order to promote the goals of conciliation in relation to their respective histories.

iv.   These programs may include developing appropriate ways of commemorating those villages and communities that existed prior to 1949.

Prime Minister Ariel Sharon's Four-Stage Disengagement Plan

Four-stage disengagement plan—Key principles

I. **Background—Diplomatic and security significance**

The State of Israel is committed to the peace process and endeavors to reach an agreed arrangement based on the vision presented by U.S. President George W. Bush.

The State of Israel believes it must take action to improve the current situation. The State of Israel has reached the conclusion that there is currently no partner on the Palestinian side with whom progress can be made on a bilateral process. Given this, a four-stage disengagement plan has been drawn up, based on the following considerations:

A. The stalemate embodied in the current situation is damaging; in order to break the stalemate, the State of Israel must initiate a process that is not dependent on cooperation with the Palestinians.

B. The aim of the plan is to bring about a better security, diplomatic economic and demographic reality.

C. In any future permanent arrangement, there will be no Israeli presence in the Gaza Strip. On the other hand, it is clear that some parts of Judea and Samaria (including key concentrations of Jewish settlements, civilian communities, security zones and areas in which Israel has a vested interest) will remain part of the State of Israel.

D. The State of Israel supports the efforts of the United States, which is working along with the international community, to promote the process of reform, the establishment of institutions and improving the economic and welfare conditions of the Palestinian people, so that a new Palestinian leadership can arise, capable of proving it can fulfill its obligations under the road map.

E. The withdrawal from the Gaza Strip and from the northern part of Samaria will reduce interaction with the Palestinian population.

F. Completion of the four-stage disengagement plan will negate any claims on Israel regarding its responsibility for the Palestinian population of the Gaza Strip.

G. The process of graduated disengagement does not detract from existing agreements between Israel and the Palestinians. The relevant security arrangements will remain in force.

H. International support for the four-stage disengagement plan is widespread and important. This support is vital in ensuring that the Palestinians fulfill their obligations in terms of fighting terror and implementing reforms, in accordance with the road map. Only then will the sides be able to resume negotiations.

II. Key points of the plan
A. The Gaza Strip
1. The State of Israel will withdraw from the Gaza Strip, including all Israeli settlements, and will redeploy outside the area of the Strip. The method of the withdrawal, with the

exception of a military presence in the area adjacent to the border between Gaza and Egypt (the Philadelphi route), will be detailed below.

2. Once the move has been completed, there will be no permanent Israeli military presence in the evacuated territorial area of the Gaza Strip.

3. As a result of this, there will be no basis to the claim that the Strip is occupied land.

B. Judea and Samaria

1. The State of Israel will withdraw from northern Samaria (four settlements: Ganim, Kadim, Sa-Nur and Homesh) as well as all permanent military installations in the area, and will redeploy outside the evacuated area.

2. Once the move has been completed, there will be no permanent Israeli military presence in the area.

3. The move will provide Palestinian territorial contiguity in the northern parts of Samaria.

4. The State of Israel, along with the international community, will help improve the transportation infrastructure in Judea and Samaria, with the goal of providing continuous transport for Palestinians in Judea and Samaria.

5. The move will make it easier for Palestinians to live a normal life in Judea and Samaria, and will facilitate economic and commercial activity.

C. The Process

The withdrawal process is slated to end by the end of 2005.

The settlements will be split into the following four groups:

1. Group A – Morag, Netzarim, Kfar Darom

2. Group B – The four settlements in northern Samaria (Ganim, Kadim, Sa-Nur and Homesh).

3. Group C – The Gush Katif bloc of settlements.

4. Group D – The settlements in the northern Gaza Strip (Alei Sinai, Dugit and Nissanit)

The necessary preparations will be undertaken in order to implement the four-stage disengagement plan (including administrative work to set relevant criteria, definitions and preparation of the necessary legislation).

The government will discuss and decide separately on the evacuation of each of the above-mentioned groups.

D. The security fence

The State of Israel will continue to construct the security fence, in accordance with the relevant cabinet decisions. In deciding on the route of the fence, humanitarian considerations will be taken into account.

III. The security reality after the evacuation

A. The Gaza Strip

1. The State of Israel will monitor and supervise the outer envelope on land, will have exclusive control of the Gaza airspace, and will continue its military activity along the Gaza Strip's coastline.

2. The Gaza Strip will be completely demilitarized of arms banned by current agreements between the sides.

3. The State of Israel reserves the basic right to self defense, which includes taking preventive measures as well as the use of force against threats originating in the Gaza Strip.

B. The West Bank

1. After the evacuation of the northern Samaria settlements, there will be no permanent military presence in that area.

2. The State of Israel reserves the basic right to self defense, which includes taking preventive measures as well as the use of force against threats originating in the area.

3. Military activity will remain in its current framework in the rest of the West Bank. The State of Israel will, if circumstances allow, consider reducing its activity in Palestinian cities.

4. The State of Israel will work to reduce the number of checkpoints throughout the West Bank.

IV. **Military infrastructure and installations in the Gaza Strip and the northern Samaria region**

All will be dismantled and evacuated, except for those that the State of Israel decides to transfer to an authorized body.

V. **The nature of the security assistance to the Palestinians**

The State of Israel agrees that in coordination with it, consulting, assistance and training will be provided to Palestinian security forces for the purpose of fighting terror and maintaining the public order. The assistance will be provided by American, British, Egyptian, Jordanian or other experts, as will be agreed upon with Israel.

The State of Israel stresses that it will not agree to any foreign security presence in Gaza or the West Bank without its consent.

VI. **The border area between the Strip and Egypt (the Philadelphi route)**

The State of Israel will continue to maintain military presence along the border between the Gaza Strip and Egypt (the Philadelphi route.) This presence is an essential security requirement. The physical widening of the route where the military activity will take place, may be necessary in certain areas.

The possibility of evacuating the area will be considered later on. This evacuation would be conditioned, among other factors, on the security reality and on the level of cooperation by Egypt in creating an alternative credible arrangement.

If and when the conditions are met enabling the evacuation of the area, the State of Israel will be willing to consider the possibility of setting up an airport and a seaport in the Gaza Strip, subject to arrangements agreed upon with the State of Israel.

VII. **Real estate**

In general, houses belonging to the settlers, and other sensitive structures such as synagogues will not be left behind. The State of Israel will aspire to transfer other structures, such as industrial and agricultural facilities, to an international third party that will use them for the benefit of the Palestinian population.

The Erez industrial zone will be transferred to an agreed-upon Palestinian or international body.

The State of Israel along with Egypt will examine the possibility of setting up a joint industrial zone on the border between Israel, Egypt and the Gaza Strip.

VIII. Infrastructure and civilian arrangements

The water, electricity, sewage and communications infrastructures will be left in place.

As a rule, Israel will enable the continued supply of electricity, water, gas and fuel to the Palestinians, under the existing arrangements and full compensation.

The existing arrangements, including the arrangements with regard to water and the electromagnetic area, will remain valid.

IX. The activity of the international civilian organizations

The State of Israel views very favorably continued activity of the international humanitarian organizations and those that deal will civil development, which aid the Palestinian population.

The State of Israel will coordinate with the international organizations the arrangements that will make this activity easier.

The State of Israel suggests that an international mechanism (such as the AHLC) be set up, in coordination with Israel and international bodies, that will work to develop the Palestinian economy.

X. Economic arrangements

In general, the economic arrangements that are currently in effect between Israel and the Palestinians will remain valid. These arrangements include, among other things:

A. The movement of goods between the Gaza Strip, Judea and Samaria, Israel and foreign countries.

B. The monetary regime.

C. The taxation arrangements and the customs envelope.

D. Postal and communications arrangements.

H. The entry of workers into Israel in accordance with the existing criteria.

In the long run, and in accordance with the Israeli interest in encouraging Palestinian economic independence, the State of Israel aspires to reduce the number of Palestinian workers entering Israel, and eventually to completely stop their entrance. The State of Israel will support the development of employment sources in the Gaza Strip and in the Palestinian areas in the West Bank, by international bodies.

XI. The international crossing points

A. The international crossing point between the Gaza Strip and Egypt

1. The existing arrangements will remain in force.

2. Israel is interested in transferring the crossing point to the "border triangle," south of its current location. This will be done in coordination with the Egyptian government. This will allow the expansion of the hours of activity at the crossing point.

B. The international crossing points between Judea and Samaria, and Jordan.

The existing arrangements will remain in force.

XII. The Erez crossing point

The Erez crossing point will be moved into the territory of the State of Israel according to a timetable that will be determined separately.

XIII. Summary

The implementation of the four-stage disengagement plan will bring about an improvement in the situation and a break from the current stagnation. If and when the Palestinian side shows a willingness, an ability and an implementation of actions to fight terrorism, a full cessation of terror and violence and the carrying out of reforms according to the road map, it will be possible to return to the track of discussions and negotiations.

U.S.-Israel Understandings

1. Letter from President George W. Bush to Prime Minister Ariel Sharon, 14 April 2004

His Excellency
Ariel Sharon
Prime Minister of Israel

Dear Mr. Prime Minister:

Thank you for your letter setting out your disengagement plan.

The United States remains hopeful and determined to find a way forward toward a resolution of the Israeli-Palestinian dispute. I remain committed to my June 24, 2002 vision of two states living side by side in peace and security as the key to peace, and to the roadmap as the route to get there.

We welcome the disengagement plan you have prepared, under which Israel would withdraw certain military installations and all settlements from Gaza, and withdraw certain military installations and settlements in the West Bank.

These steps described in the plan will mark real progress toward realizing my June 24, 2002 vision, and make a real contribution towards peace. We also understand that, in this context, Israel believes it is important to bring new opportunities to the Negev and the Galilee. We are hopeful that steps pursuant to this plan, consistent with my vision, will remind all states and parties of their own obligations under the roadmap.

The United States appreciates the risks such an undertaking represents. I therefore want to reassure you on several points.

First, the United States remains committed to my vision and to its implementation as described in the roadmap. The United States will do its utmost to prevent any attempt by anyone to impose any other plan. Under the roadmap, Palestinians must undertake an immediate cessation of armed activity and all acts of violence against Israelis anywhere, and all official Palestinian institutions must end incitement against Israel. The Palestinian leadership must act decisively against terror, including sustained, targeted, and effective operations to stop terrorism and dismantle terrorist capabilities and infrastructure. Palestinians must undertake a comprehensive and fundamental political reform that includes a strong parliamentary democracy and an empowered prime minister.

Second, there will be no security for Israelis or Palestinians until they and all states, in the region and beyond, join together to fight terrorism and dismantle terrorist organizations. The United States reiterates its steadfast commitment to Israel's security, including secure, defensible borders, and to preserve and strengthen Israel's capability to deter and defend itself, by itself, against any threat or possible combination of threats.

Third, Israel will retain its right to defend itself against terrorism, including to take actions against terrorist organizations. The United States will lead efforts, working together with Jordan, Egypt, and others in the international community, to build the capacity and will of Palestinian institutions to fight terrorism, dismantle terrorist organizations, and prevent the areas from which Israel has withdrawn from posing a threat that would have to be addressed by any other means. The United States understands that after Israel withdraws from Gaza and/or parts of the West Bank, and pending agreements on other arrangements, existing arrangements regarding control of airspace, territorial waters, and land passages of the West Bank and Gaza will continue. The United States is strongly committed to Israel's security and well-being as a Jewish state. It seems clear that an agreed, just, fair, and realistic framework for a solution to the Palestinian refugee issue as part of any final status agreement will need to be found through the establishment of a Palestinian state, and the settling of Palestinian refugees there, rather than in Israel.

As part of a final peace settlement, Israel must have secure and recognized borders, which should emerge from negotiations between the parties in accordance with UNSC Resolutions 242 and 338. In light of new realities on the ground, including already existing major Israeli populations centers, it is unrealistic to expect that the outcome of final status negotiations will be a full and complete return to the armistice lines of 1949, and all previous efforts to negotiate a two-state solution have reached the same conclusion. It is realistic to expect that any final status agreement will only be achieved on the basis of mutually agreed changes that reflect these realities.

I know that, as you state in your letter, you are aware that certain responsibilities face the State of Israel. Among these, your government has stated that the barrier being erected by Israel should be a security rather than political barrier, should be temporary rather than permanent, and therefore not prejudice any final status issues including final borders, and its route should take into account, consistent with security needs, its impact on Palestinians not engaged in terrorist activities.

As you know, the United States supports the establishment of a Palestinian state that is viable, contiguous, sovereign, and independent, so that the Palestinian people can build their own future in accordance with my vision set forth in June 2002 and with the path set forth in the roadmap. The United States will join with others in the international community to foster the development of democratic political institutions and new leadership committed to those institutions, the reconstruction of civic institutions, the growth of a free and prosperous economy, and the building of capable security institutions dedicated to maintaining law and order and dismantling terrorist organizations.

A peace settlement negotiated between Israelis and Palestinians would be a great boon not only to those peoples but to the peoples of the entire region. Accordingly, the United States believes that all states in the region have special responsibilities: to support the building of the institutions of a Palestinian state; to fight terrorism, and cut off all forms of assistance to individuals and groups engaged in terrorism; and to begin now to move toward more normal relations with the State of Israel. These actions would be true contributions to building peace in the region.

Mr. Prime Minister, you have described a bold and historic initiative that can make an important contribution to peace. I commend your efforts and your courageous decision which I support. As a close friend and ally, the United States intends to work closely with you to help make it a success.

Sincerely,

George W. Bush

2. Letter from Dov Weissglas, Chief of the Prime Minister's Bureau to
National Security Adviser, Dr. Condoleezza Rice, 18 April 2004

Dr. Condoleezza Rice
National Security Adviser
The White House
Washington, D.C.

Dear Dr. Rice,

On behalf of the Prime Minister of the State of Israel, Mr. Ariel Sharon,
I wish to reconfirm the following understanding, which had been reached
between us:

1. Restrictions on settlement growth: within the agreed principles of
settlement activities, an effort will be made in the next few days to have a
better definition of the construction line of settlements in Judea & Samaria.
An Israeli team, in conjunction with Ambassador Kurtzer, will review aerial
photos of settlements and will jointly define the construction line of each of
the settlements.

2. Removal of unauthorized outposts: the Prime Minister and the Minister of
Defense, jointly, will prepare a list of unauthorized outposts with indicative
dates of their removal; the Israeli Defense forces and/or the Israeli Police will
take continuous action to remove those outposts in the targeted dates. The
said list will be presented to Ambassador Kurtzer within 30 days.

3. Mobility restrictions in Judea & Samaria: the Minister of Defense will
provide Ambassador Kurtzer with a map indicating roadblocks and other
transportational barriers posed across Judea & Samaria. A list of barriers
already removed and a timetable for further removals will be included
in this list. Needless to say, the matter of the existence of transportational
barriers fully depends on the current security situation and might be changed
accordingly.

4. Legal attachments of Palestinian revenues: the matter is pending in various
courts of law in Israel, awaiting judicial decisions. We will urge the State

Attorney's office to take any possible legal measure to expedite the rendering of those decisions.

5. The Government of Israel extends to the Government of the United States the following assurances:

a. The Israeli government remains committed to the two-state solution— Israel and Palestine living side by side in peace and security—as the key to peace in the Middle East.

b. The Israeli government remains committed to the Roadmap as the only route to achieving the two-state solution.

c. The Israeli government believes that its disengagement plan and related steps on the West Bank concerning settlement growth, unauthorized outposts, and easing of restrictions on the movement of Palestinians not engaged in terror are consistent with the Roadmap and, in many cases, are steps actually called for in certain phases of the Roadmap.

d. The Israeli government believes that further steps by it, even if consistent with the Roadmap, cannot be taken absent the emergence of a Palestinian partner committed to peace, democratic reform, and the fight against terror.

e. Once such a Palestinian partner emerges, the Israeli government will perform its obligations, as called for in the Roadmap, as part of the performance-based plan set out in the Roadmap for reaching a negotiated final status agreement.

f. The Israeli government remains committed to the negotiation between the parties of a final status resolution of all outstanding issues.

g. The Government of Israel supports the United States' efforts to reform the Palestinian security services to meet their roadmap obligations to fight terror. Israel also supports the American efforts, working with the international community, to promote the reform process, build institutions, and improve the economy of the Palestinian Authority and to enhance the welfare of its people, in the hope that a new Palestinian leadership will prove able to fulfill its obligations under the Roadmap. The Israeli Government will take all reasonable actions requested by these parties to facilitate these efforts.

h. As the Government of Israel has stated, the barrier being erected by Israel should be a security rather than a political barrier, should be temporary rather than permanent, and therefore not prejudice any final status issues including final borders, and its route should take into account, consistent with security needs, its impact on Palestinians not engaged in terrorist activities.

Sincerely,

Dov Weissglas
Chief of the Prime Minister's Bureau

Index

Abed Rabbo, Yasser, 111, 157, 160
Abu Mazen (Mahmoud Abbas),
    124–25, 135, 140–42, 145–47,
    152, 162
Abu Ala (Ahmed Qurei), 60, 111
airspace, 46, 47, 50, 54, 57, 100, 139,
    212, 219
Al-Aksa Intifada, 18, 47–48, 82, 86,
    113, 154
Americans, 5, 27, 31, 33, 39, 42, 45,
    47, 50, 54, 67, 89–90, 107, 109,
    111, 116, 122–23, 125, 133, 155
Arab League, 69–70, 77–78, 84, 90,
    94, 103–4, 141, 146, 158, 187,
    190
Arab League Resolution, 77–78, 84,
    90, 94, 103, 104, 146

Arafat, Yasser, 4, 153–54, 156, 160,
    165, 167–68
autonomy, 3–4, 15, 24, 39
Ayalon, Ami, 114, 117, 160

Barak, Ehud, 24, 33, 155
Beilin, Yossi, 55, 59, 61, 91, 155,
    157
Ben-Ami, Shlomo, 55
Bertini Report, 80, 91, 193
borders, 3, 5–6, 14, 17–18, 23,
    38–40, 42, 45–46, 49, 56, 70–71,
    74, 82–83, 85–87, 91, 96–97, 100,
    106, 115–16, 123, 133, 138, 143–
    44, 159, 194–96, 218–19, 223
Bush, George W., 73, 209, 217,
    220

Camp David, 15, 37–48, 152, 155–56, 160–62

cease-fire, 67

Clinton Parameters, 49–54

Clinton, Bill, 27, 32, 37–38, 45–51, 53–55, 57, 59–61, 73, 94, 99–101, 103, 106–08, 113, 115–16, 139, 153, 155–57

Convergence Plan, 147, 164

Crown Prince Abdullah, 69, 190

demilitarization, 46, 139

Demirel, Suleyman, 63

DFLP, 24

Dayton, General Keith, 125

Disengagement Plan, 119–31, 139, 209–10, 212, 215, 217, 222

Declaration of Principles (OOP), see Oslo Accords Egypt

Egyptians, 125

EU, 56, 125, 156–57, 187, 189, 203

Fatah, 4, 10, 95, 114, 124, 143, 145–46, 164

Fence, see separation barrier, wall/fence

Gaza, 1, 4, 5, 9, 12–13, 16–21, 23, 24–25, 27, 32, 34, 39–40, 46–48, 57, 97, 99, 112, 115, 119, 121–27, 129, 132–33, 137–38, 145–46, 149, 153–54, 157, 161, 163, 167, 169–181, 183, 186, 194, 210, 212–15, 217, 219

Geneva Accord, 92–113, 115–17, 121–22, 139–40, 199–207

Gulf War, 12

Hamas, 20, 25, 124, 141, 143–47, 163–64

Haniye, Ismail, 145–46

Hebron, 14, 21, 25–31, 33, 64, 97, 109

Hebron Protocol, see Oslo Accords

holy sites, 23, 59, 96

humanitarian measures, 79–80

incitement, 28, 30–31, 64, 88, 101, 129, 155, 191, 218

Interim Agreement, see Oslo Accords

international conference, 82–84, 149, 195–96

Intifada Iran,

Islamic Jihad, 20, 25, 124

Jangland, Thorbjoern, 63

Jericho, 13, 17–21, 23–24, 154, 171, 174, 176–77, 183

Jerusalem

  Abu Dis, 45

  Armenian Quarter, 107–08, 157

  East Jerusalem, 3–4, 21, 24–25, 28–29, 34, 38–39, 42, 45, 48, 57, 59, 69, 79, 111, 114, 127,

138, 141, 156, 159, 163, 185–86, 193

West Jerusalem, 3, 4, 42, 106, 156

Haram al-Sharif, 27, 38, 45–46, 53, 59, 96, 105, 107–08, 110, 116, 140, 154, 160

holy sites, 23, 59, 96

Jewish Quarter, 42, 45, 107–08

Old City, 3, 39, 42, 45–46, 106–08

Temple Mount, 27, 38–39, 45–46, 48, 53, 59, 96, 106–08, 110, 116, 140, 160

Jordan, 4, 10, 21, 27, 29, 34, 39, 50, 53, 57, 70, 75, 81, 91, 99–100, 122, 138, 141, 152, 157, 161, 163, 173, 192, 215, 218

Jordan Rift Valley, 39

Kadima, 146, 163

King Hussein Labor Party

land swaps, *see* swaps

Lebanon, 1, 3, 5, 10, 51, 59, 70, 82, 84, 91, 149, 157–58, 186, 195–96, 201

Likud Party, 137

Lipkin-Shahak, General Amnon, 55

Livni, Tzipi, 144

Madrid Conference, 12, 82, 153, 185, 190

Meretz Party, 125

Mitchell, Senator George, 63

Mitchell Committee, 66–68, 74, 76, 78, 81, 85, 89

Mitchell Report, 68, 191, 194

monitoring, 30, 32, 34, 68, 80–83, 87–88, 91, 95–96, 100, 108–09, 192, 194, 196

National Religious Party negotiations,

Netanyahu, Binyamin, 26–33, 75

Norway, 105, 159, 167, 203

Nusseibeh, Sari, 114

Nusseibeh-Ayalon Petition, 112–13

Olmert, Ehud, 143

Oslo Accords, 5, 9–35, 42, 48, 56, 78–79, 81, 85–87, 95, 101, 111, 122, 137, 144, 152

OOP

exchange of letters, 133

Hebron Protocol, 27–29

Interim Agreement, 13, 17, 20–21, 23, 25–29, 32, 85, 87, 91, 119, 172–73, 182

Oslo II, 13, 20, 22–23, 87

Paris Agreement

Wye River Memorandum

outposts

Palestine, 2–5, 9–10, 18, 39–40, 51, 63, 71, 74, 78–79, 84–85, 94–97, 99–101, 103–06, 108–09, 111, 114–16, 123, 138, 141, 143, 145,

149, 151–57, 159–60, 164, 197, 199–202, 206, 222
Palestine National Council (PNC), 10
Palestinian Authority (PA), 17–18, 20, 24, 42, 51, 74, 76, 82, 88–89, 91, 94, 111, 143, 145, 147, 157, 159, 177, 191, 222
Palestinian Legislative Council (PLC), 26
Palestinian state, 5, 9, 11, 27, 29, 38–40, 45–47, 50–51, 53–54, 57, 59, 69, 71, 73–75, 77, 78, 82–83, 85–87, 91, 94, 97, 99, 103, 115, 117, 127, 132, 138–139, 153, 157, 185–86, 190–92, 194–96, 219–20
Paris Agreement, *see* Oslo Accords
Peres, Shimon, 26, 154
PFLP, 24
Philadelphi Corridor, 122, 124
PLO, 4–5, 9–15, 20–21, 24–26, 28, 32, 53, 94, 114, 137, 145–47, 153–56, 163, 165–68
PNC, 26, 32, 154
police prisoners

Quartet, 77, 81–84, 86–89, 91, 95, 105, 125, 135, 145, 159, 189–90, 192, 194–96
Rabin, Yitzhak, 5, 12, 14, 165, 168
Redeployment, *see also* withdrawal
refugees, 3, 6, 15, 17, 38, 40, 42, 47, 51, 59–61, 69–71, 82, 84, 90, 102–05, 110–11, 114–16, 139–41,

157, 171, 195–96, 199–201, 203–06, 209
Report of the Sharm el-Sheikh Fact-finding Committee (Mitchell Report),
Rice, Condoleezza, 133, 221
right of return, 40, 47, 51, 54, 60, 70, 90, 102–03, 110, 114–17, 140
Road Map, 76, 78–90, 92–95, 99, 122–23, 130, 132, 135, 139, 145, 156, 158–59, 162–63, 189–97, 210, 215
Rose Garden Speech, 73–77, 86, 94
Rudman, Warren, 63
Russia, 77, 163, 189

Sadat, Anwar, 14, 69
safe-passage, 28
Sarid, Yossi, 55
Saudi Arabia, 69, 116, 158, 185
Saudi Initiative, *see also* Arab League Resolution
security, 6, 10–11, 14–17, 19, 21, 23, 25–26, 30–32, 34, 38–40, 42, 46, 50–51, 53, 57, 63–68, 74–75, 78–82, 84–86, 92–93, 95–96, 99–102, 107–08, 114–17, 119, 121, 123–25, 133, 135, 138–39, 144–46, 165–66, 169–72, 174, 177, 183, 186, 189–97, 209–10, 212–13, 217–19, 222–23
self-determination, 2, 4, 15
separation barrier, 87, 119, 132–33, 138, 144, 159, 161, 163

settlers11, 20, 23–25, 34, 39, 46, 50,
  56–57, 80, 97, 115, 127, 129, 152,
  213
settlements, 17–18, 21, 23–25, 27,
  34, 46, 48, 56, 64, 66, 68, 80–81,
  83–84, 87, 104, 106, 115–116,
  119, 121–22, 126–29, 131–33,
  138–39, 141–42, 144, 152, 157,
  161–63, 171, 177, 181, 183, 194–
  96, 202, 210–12, 217, 221
Sha'ath, Nebil, 59
Sharansky, Natan, 75
Sharon, Ariel, 24, 126–27, 137, 141,
  209, 217, 221
Solana, Javier, 63
sovereignty, 39–40, 45–46, 50–51,
  53, 59, 74, 91, 96, 99–100, 106–
  08, 110, 116, 140, 194, 200
Soviet Union, 4, 10, 12, 152
swaps, 39, 48, 50, 56–57, 59, 97, 99,
  103, 115, 138
Switzerland, 105, 203
Syria, 3–4, 10, 12, 33, 35, 78, 82,
  84, 91, 153, 157–58, 186, 190,
  195–96

Taba, 54, 55–61, 70, 87, 93–94, 103,
  113, 132, 157
Temple Mount/Haram el-sharif, see
  Jerusalem
Temporary International Presence
  (TIP, TIPH), 20, 27
Tenet, George, 32, 67, 155
Tenet Plan, 67–68, 78–79, 85

terror, 10, 14, 25–26, 28, 56, 67–68,
  73, 76, 88, 93, 135, 141, 145, 154,
  190, 192, 194, 210, 213, 215, 218,
  222
terrorism, 5, 20, 24–26, 28–31, 34,
  64, 66, 68, 70, 73–75, 78–79, 81,
  87, 96, 101, 108–09, 121, 123–24,
  126, 133, 166–67, 189, 191–92,
  215, 218–20, 223

United Nations (UN), 3, 77, 165,
  187, 189, 203
  Resolution 181 (Partition Plan),
    3, 71, 159
  Resolution 194, 40, 42, 51, 60,
    70–71, 84, 90, 102, 139, 186
  Resolution 242, 4–5, 10, 14–16,
    18, 69, 71, 90–91, 115, 153, 199
  Resolution 338, 71
  Resolution 1397, 69–71, 77, 90
United States (US), 6, 10, 12, 29–31,
  37, 71, 74, 77, 81, 85, 88, 93, 101,
  130–33, 152, 175, 183, 187, 189,
  203, 210, 217–23
UNRWA, 104–05, 203–06

Wakf, 109
Wall/fence
Ward, General William, 125
water, 17, 46, 48, 56, 80, 82, 107,
  109, 122, 125, 139, 161, 172, 178,
  180, 195, 214, 219
weapons, 12, 24–25, 28, 30–32, 34,
  65, 79, 101–102, 123, 155, 192

WITHDRAWN

Weissglas, Dov, 133, 221, 223
West Bank, 3–5, 9, 11–13, 16–22,
   23–25, 27–30, 32, 34, 39–40, 46,
   48–49, 56–57, 65, 68, 70, 86, 91,
   93, 97, 99–100, 115, 119, 121–23,
   125–27, 129, 132–33, 137–38,
   141, 143–46, 151, 153–54,
   156–57, 161, 163, 167, 169–75,
   177–81, 186, 194, 212–13, 215,
   217, 219, 222
withdrawal, 1, 4–5, 17–19, 21,
   23–24, 26–27, 29–31, 33, 53, 57,
   68–69, 71, 78, 87, 89, 95, 97, 99,
   102, 107–09, 112, 119, 122–24,
      126–27, 129, 138, 154, 164,
      171, 174, 176, 182–83, 185–86,
      210–11
Wolfensohn, James, 125
World Bank, 105, 125, 159, 161, 203
Wye River Memorandum *see* Oslo
   Accords
Yom Kippur War, 71
Zinni, George, 67–69, 73
Zionism, 2, 90, 95
1948 war, 42, 91
1967 war (Six Day War), 3–4, 21, 42,
   45, 91